SOURCES, STORIES, AND SONGS

ANTHOLOGY

W9-COE-274

A Young Nation

ADVENTURES IN TIME AND PLACE

- Biographies and Autobiographies
- Diaries and Journals
- Essays
- Fiction and Nonfiction Selections
- Folk Tales and Legends
- Interviews
- Letters
- Newspaper Articles
- Plays
- Poems
- Songs
- Speeches
- Visual Documents

McGraw-Hill
School Division
New York   Farmington

PROGRAM AUTHORS

Dr. James A. Banks
Professor of Education and
    Director of the Center for
    Multicultural Education
University of Washington
Seattle, Washington

Dr. Barry K. Beyer
Professor Emeritus, Graduate
    School of Education
George Mason University
Fairfax, Virginia

Dr. Gloria Contreras
Professor of Education
University of North Texas
Denton, Texas

Jean Craven
District Coordinator of
    Curriculum Development
Albuquerque Public Schools
Albuquerque, New Mexico

Dr. Gloria Ladson-Billings
Professor of Education
University of Wisconsin
Madison, Wisconsin

Dr. Mary A. McFarland
Instructional Coordinator of
    Social Studies, K–12, and
    Director of Staff Development
Parkway School District
Chesterfield, Missouri

Dr. Walter C. Parker
Professor and Program Chair for
    Social Studies Education
University of Washington
Seattle, Washington

Acknowledgments

"The Beautiful Dream" from AND IT IS STILL THAT WAY by Byrd Baylor. ©1976 by Byrd Baylor. Published by Trails West Press, Santa Fe, NM.

"The Conquistadors Search for Gold" from THE BROKEN SPEARS: THE AZTEC ACCOUNT OF THE CONQUEST OF MEXICO by Miguel Leon-Portilla. ©1962 by Beacon Press, Boston.

"Two Views on Women's Rights" from THE BOOK OF ABIGAIL AND JOHN: SELECTED LETTERS OF THE ADAMS FAMILY 1762–1784. L. H. Butterfield, editor, Cambridge, MA; Harvard University Press. ©1975 by the Massachusetts Historical Society.

"Sweet Betsy from Pike" and "Erie Canal" from MUSIC AND YOU, Senior Authors: Barbara Merrill Staton. ©1991 Macmillan Publishing Company, a division of Macmillan, Inc.

"Reaching the Americas" from THE LOG OF CHRISTOPHER COLUMBUS, by Robert H. Fuson. ©1987 by Robert H. Fuson. Published by International Marine, an imprint of TAB Books, a Division of McGraw-Hill Inc., Blue Ridge Summit, PA 17294-0850.

"Save the Earth (It's Not Too Late)" by Professor Rap. ©1990 Professor Rap.

(continued on page 124)

McGraw-Hill School Division

A Division of The McGraw-Hill Companies

McGraw-Hill School Division
1221 Avenue of the Americas
New York, New York 10020

Printed in the United States of America

ISBN 0-02-148295-0

4 5 6 7 8 9 066 03 02 01 00 99

TABLE OF Contents

= audiocassette

USING PRIMARY SOURCES AND LITERATURE WITH SOCIAL STUDIES

The readings in the *Adventures in Time and Place Anthology* have been carefully selected to enhance Social Studies concepts and to provide enjoyable and worthwhile reading experiences for students. All readers bring to the reading experience their own backgrounds and prior knowledge. Exposing students to a variety of viewpoints while encouraging them to question and ponder what they read will help them to become critical readers and thoughtful citizens.

The readings include **primary sources, secondary sources,** and **literature.** These fall into several categories and include:

- songs
- official documents
- oral histories
- posters
- diaries and journals
- photographs and graphics
- interviews
- political cartoons
- poems
- folk tales
- letters
- autobiographies and biographies
- newspaper articles
- fiction and nonfiction
- personal recollections
- speeches

The readings offer you a unique teaching tool. The following suggestions will help your students use the readings to build and extend their knowledge of social studies as well as to sharpen their analytical skills.

PRIMARY AND SECONDARY SOURCES

A **primary source** is something that comes from the time that is being studied. Primary sources include such things as official documents of the time, diaries and journals, letters, newspaper articles and advertisements, photographs, and oral histories. A **secondary source** is an account of the past written by someone who was not an eyewitness to those events. Remind students of the difference between primary and secondary sources. Point out that primary sources give historians valuable clues from the past because they provide first-hand information about a certain time or event. Primary sources let the reader see how people lived, felt, and thought.

However, primary sources express the view of only one person. Thus, it is important for students to understand the point of view of the writer and to find out all that they can about his or her background to decide whether the writer is credible, or believable. Secondary sources often compare and analyze different points of view and give a broader view of the event, but once again it is important for students to understand the writer's point of view and analyze his or her credentials. Suggest to students that when they read primary and secondary sources, they ask themselves these questions:

- Who created the source?
- Can the writer be believed?
- Does the writer have expert knowledge of the subject?
- Does the writer have a reason to describe the events in a certain way?
- Does the writer have a reputation for being accurate?

When you work with the primary sources in this Anthology, you may wish to encourage students to think about the following as they read some of the various sources:

Diaries and Journals Was the diary or journal originally written to be shared with the public?

Speeches Was the intent of the speech to persuade the audience to adopt a particular point of view or was the speech merely informative?

Newspaper Articles Did the newspaper in which the article appeared have a particular political stance or bias that might have influenced the writer?

Official Documents Are there any words or phrases in the document that you do not understand? If so, what other source can you consult for clarification?

LITERATURE

In Social Studies, literature is used to motivate and instruct. It also plays a large role in assisting students to understand their cultural heritage and the cultural heritage of others. For example, the folk tales included in the *Adventures in Time and Place Anthology* were chosen from a wide range of cultures to offer students a glimpse of the wisdom various cultures deem important to impart. The songs, stories, and poetry of different cultures offer students an opportunity to compare and contrast and hence understand aspects of cultural identity.

Well-written historical fiction can not only give students a chance to observe historical events from the perspective of someone close to their own age, but it can also provide motivation for students to read more about the events described. For example, *Johnny Tremain* by Esther Forbes has long motivated students to learn more about the American Revolution.

USING YOUR *Anthology*

In *A Young Nation* you will be reading about many different people, places, and times. This Anthology, or collection of documents created by different people, will make the information in your textbook come to life in a special way. Some of the documents are letters, stories, diaries, songs, poems, and political essays. Others are items you might not have thought of as documents, such as old advertisements, posters, illustrations, photographs, and even a buffalo hide. As you study these documents, you will be able to see, feel, and hear what it was like to live in other times and places. The documents in the Anthology will help you to better understand the story of our country and the people who helped to build it.

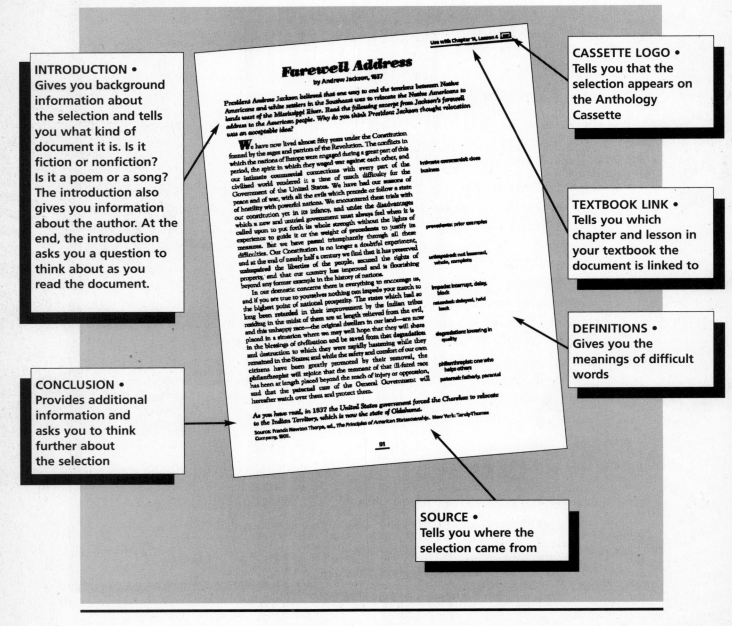

INTRODUCTION •
Gives you background information about the selection and tells you what kind of document it is. Is it fiction or nonfiction? Is it a poem or a song? The introduction also gives you information about the author. At the end, the introduction asks you a question to think about as you read the document.

CONCLUSION •
Provides additional information and asks you to think further about the selection

CASSETTE LOGO •
Tells you that the selection appears on the Anthology Cassette

TEXTBOOK LINK •
Tells you which chapter and lesson in your textbook the document is linked to

DEFINITIONS •
Gives you the meanings of difficult words

SOURCE •
Tells you where the selection came from

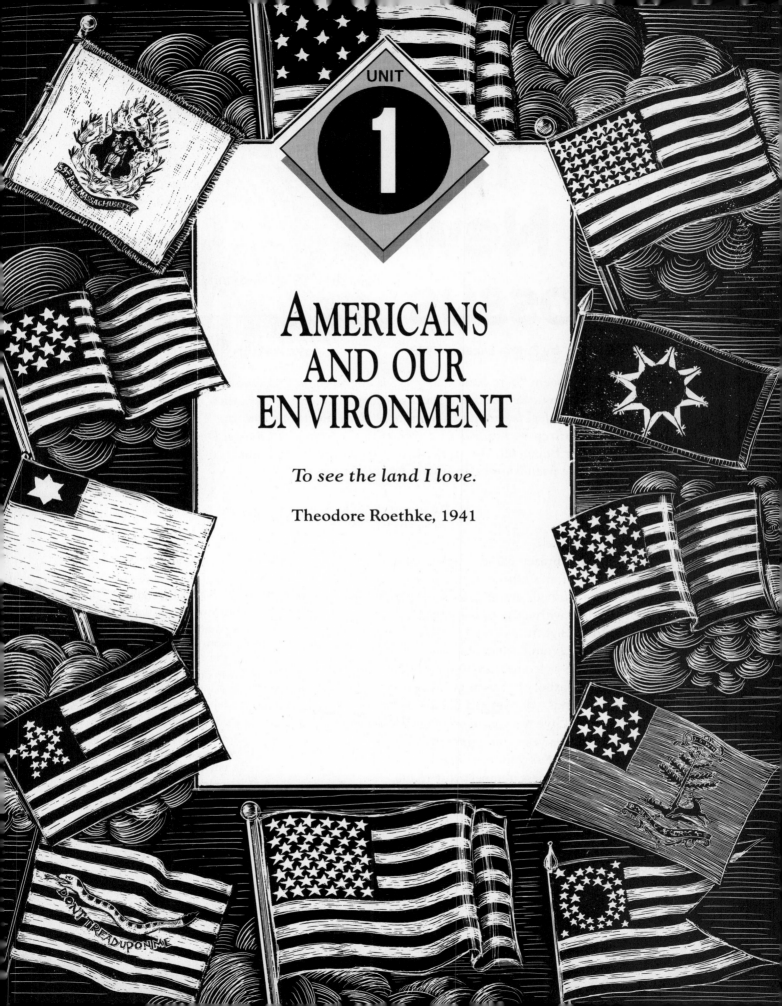

UNIT

1

AMERICANS
AND OUR
ENVIRONMENT

To see the land I love.

Theodore Roethke, 1941

The New Colossus

by Emma Lazarus, 1883

Emma Lazarus's poem "The New Colossus" is engraved on a plaque inside the Statue of Liberty. The poem celebrates the spirit of acceptance and appreciation of diverse cultures that many feel is the most remarkable thing about our country. "The New Colossus" was written by Lazarus as a tribute to the Statue of Liberty. Designed by Frederic-Auguste Bartholdi, the statue was given to the United States in 1886 by France, as a symbol of the friendship between the two countries.

Not like the **brazen** giant of Greek fame,
With conquering limbs astride from land to land;
Here at our sea-washed, sunset gates shall stand
A mighty woman with a torch, whose flame
Is the imprisoned lightning, and her name
Mother of **Exiles**. From her **beacon**-hand
Glows world-wide welcome; her mild eyes command
The **air-bridged harbor** that **twin cities** frame.
"Keep, ancient lands, your **storied pomp**!" cries she
With silent lips. "Give me your tired, your poor,
Your huddled masses yearning to breathe free,
The **wretched refuse** of your **teeming** shore.
Send these, the homeless, **tempest-tost** to me,
I lift my lamp beside the golden door."

brazen: bold

Exiles: people forced to leave their countries

beacon: guiding signal

air-bridged harbor: New York harbor, spanned by the Brooklyn Bridge

twin cities: Brooklyn and Manhattan, which were separate cities at the time

storied pomp: old habits and fancy ways

wretched refuse: unwanted people

teeming: swarming

tempest-tost: battered by storms

The poet compares the Statue of Liberty to the Colossus of Rhodes, a huge monument known as one of the Seven Wonders of the World. The Colossus of Rhodes was built as a symbol of the power of the mighty Greek empire. What does the "new Colossus" stand for? Why does the poet contrast the two statues?

Source: Emily Stipes Watt, ed., *The Poetry of American Women from 1632 to 1945*. Austin: University of Texas Press, 1977.

Save the EARTH (It's Not Too Late)

by Professor Rap, 1991

In the past 25 years, many Americans have become aware of the dangers of pollution. What can you do to help clean up the environment? A musician named Professor Rap has a few ideas. In 1991 he wrote a song called Save the Earth (It's Not Too Late). As you read or sing this song, notice the different types of geographic features and the forms of pollution that he mentions. What are some of Professor Rap's suggestions you can use to help save Earth?

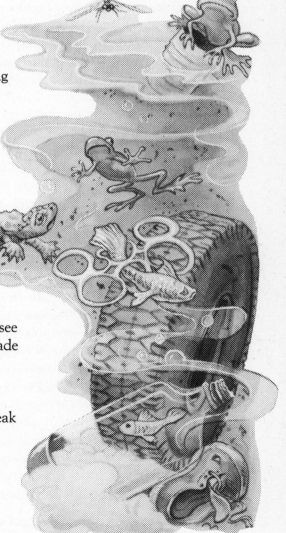

Just suppose you were a crystal blue lake and
    through bad decisions and mistakes
People filled you with things that don't belong
Now you're not so blue no more, something's wrong
'Cause people won't swim in you (that's right)
And the fish can't live in you
Your shore was once filled with sand
And now it's a garbage can
D'ya see what I'm sayin'?
It's not a game that we're playin' (no more)

(Chorus)
It's not too late
Let's not hesitate
Let us all work together
To protect the earth we treasure

Just imagine you were a beautiful green tree
And the air that's around you made you sick, you see
The kids used to climb in you, you used to give shade
    to someone reading a book on a lazy Saturday
Now the kids can't climb in you, your
    limbs have gone weak
You can't give shade no more, if only you could speak
The birds can't nest in you, do you see
    what I'm sayin'?
We've got to start living right, it's not a
    game we're playing

(Chorus)

Now, if we all work together, and get involved
Our environmental problems will one day be solved
No we're not preaching, or blaming you alone
We just want these problems to be better known
Now, no one could ever be too educated
And to those who want to learn, this song is dedicated
So, take it from me, the hip-hop cat
You just can't argue when it comes to facts
Pollution is everywhere and often hides
In factory smokestacks and pesticides
It's time we got serious and lend a hand
With things like not using aerosol cans
The things you can do are debatable
But, it's always good to use **biodegradable**. . .
Products. . .to stop the growth of **landfills**
And help clean up the litter on the sides of our hills.
The **ozone layer** protects us from. . .
harmful rays sent down by the sun
After years of polluting, it's formed a hole
It grows every day over the South Pole
We are only adding to its growing rate
It's been said to be three times the size of the U.S.A.
To me, that's a problem, and to you it should too
It's time we decided what we want to do
It's a real scary fact, yet hardly known
We're **deteriorating** our ozone. . .
Layer upon layers of garbage sits. . .
 in landfills. . .I mean, if it fits
We need to recycle, all of us, and soon
So we can help control our planet's doom
It's as simple as that. . .ten minutes a day
And help save the next generation on the way

(Chorus)

biodegradable: able to
 be broken down by
 nature
landfills: garbage dumps
ozone layer: layer of air
 high above the earth

deteriorating: breaking
 down

Now, if everybody, from the richest to the poorest...
Helps out...we can save the rain forest
We're losing our trees, one by one
We need the trees to make oxygen
Did you know that? That's what we breathe
I like to breathe! So help out—please!
It's not going to take you that much time
You do your share and I'll do mine
Okay, but, polluted air hurt states like Maine
Where, like in many other places, has **acid rain**   **acid rain:** poisonous rain
Factory smoke can take some of the blame, (but)   caused by pollution
Laws aren't that stiff, and that's a shame
Acid rain is formed from **toxins** in the air...   **toxins:** poisons
   falling down in rain drops here and everywhere
Slowly, but surely, these things come back to haunt
Now tell me...is that what you really want?

(Chorus)

I am tired of things that make me cough
Like the smell of smoke, or car exhaust
Every day stuff adds up to ruin our planet
It's these things that we all take for granted
Unrecyclable plastic bags add up to a lot
It takes hundreds of years before they rot
And Styrofoam...we see it everyday
When you throw it out, you think it's gone, it never goes away
We've got to get serious, and want to win
So let's stick together through thick and thin
Like stop using aerosol and Styrofoam cups
Believe me, all the little things will soon add up
Be a part...set a goal and pursue it
We're in too deep to "let the other guy do it"
So...to every man, woman, boy and girl
Let's share a goal to make our earth a better world.

(Chorus)

Source: Professor Rap, *Save the Earth (It's Not Too Late)*. Utica, MI: Dalka Studios, 1991.

Night Journey

by Theodore Roethke, 1941

Seeing the United States from an airplane is very different from seeing the country from a train. From a plane, mountains, lakes, and valleys look tiny and almost like toys. Through a train window, however, the geography of the land comes to life—especially when you take a ride with the poet Theodore Roethke (reth' kē, 1908-1963). Born in Michigan, Roethke became one of the leading poets in the United States. In Night Journey, the poem below, Roethke describes a midnight train ride across the United States. As you read this poem, picture in your mind what Roethke is describing from his train window. Notice the different types of geographical features he passes. How do Roethke's words make you feel the land and the train as well as see them?

Now as the train **bears** west

Its rhythm rocks the earth,

And from my **Pullman berth**

I stare into the night

While others take their rest.

Bridges of iron lace,

A suddenness of trees,

A lap of mountain mist

bears: heads

Pullman berth:
    bed in a railroad car

All cross my line of sight,

Then a **bleak** wasted place,   **bleak:** barren

And a lake below my knees.

Full on my neck I feel

The straining at a curve;

My muscles move with steel,

I wake in every nerve.

I watch a **beacon** swing   **beacon:** signal light

From dark to blazing bright;

We thunder through **ravines**   **ravines:** steep valleys

And **gullies** washed with light.   **gullies:** dry riverbeds

Beyond the mountain pass

Mist deepens on the **pane**;   **pane:** window glass

We rush into a rain

That rattles double glass.

Wheels shake the **roadbed stone**,   **roadbed stone:** stone beneath the tracks

The **pistons** jerk and shove,   **pistons:** engine parts

I stay up half the night

To see the land I love.

Traveling by train is one of the faster ways to see the countryside. But you can also travel more slowly—by bicycle, by skateboard, or on foot. How do the feeling of movement and the look of the countryside change when you use a different form of transportation?

Source: Theodore Roethke, *The Collected Poems of Theodore Roethke*. Garden City, NY: Doubleday and Company, Inc., 1966.

An American History Textbook in the 1800s

by Emma Willard, 1869

Below is a page from a secondary source—an American history textbook. This one was written by Emma Willard (1787–1870), a leading educator of the 1800s. First published in 1828, Willard's textbook was one of the first American history textbooks in the nineteenth century. Although written at about a junior high school level, the book was used by students of all ages. Look below at the book's opening pages, which focus on history and geography. How do they look compared with your textbook? Now read the text. How is it different from your textbook? How is it similar?

Washington's Inauguration.

CHAPTER I.

Definitions, &c.

1. THE subject of this work is the United States of America; or, as those States are sometimes called, the Republic or Nation of America.

What constitutes a nation? First, there must be a country, with the natural divisions of land and water; second, there must be men, women, and children to inhabit that country; and third, those inhabitants must be bound together in one, by living under a common government, which extends its protection over all, and which all are bound to obey.

2. To every nation there belongs a *history:* For whenever the inhabitants of any large portion of the earth are united under one government, *important public events* must there have taken place. *The record of these events* constitutes the history of that country.

3. The events of history should always be recorded, with the circumstances of *time* and *place.* To tell *when* events happened, is to give their chronology;

Side notes: CHAP. I. Subject. Its triple division. Any nation's history.

1. What is the subject of this work? What three parts compose a nation?—2. What constitutes any nation's history? 3. How should events be recorded? What is it to give their chronology?

13

14   ONE NATION.

to tell *where* they happened, their geography. The history of a nation, is therefore inseparably connected with its geography and chronology. Chronology may properly be called the skeleton of history, geography the base on which it stands.

4. First, let us inquire, where is the country of which we desire to know the history? In the vast universe, is a system of planets surrounding a sun, hence called the solar system. The third planet from the sun is called the earth. On the earth's surface, the UNITED STATES OF AMERICA occupies a northern portion of the smaller of two continents. In extent, it is one of the largest nations of the world.

5. In longitude, the Republic of America ranges through sixty degrees, from the Atlantic ocean to the Pacific. In latitude, it reaches from the Cape of Florida, in north latitude twenty-five degrees, to British and Russian America in forty-nine. Thus stretching through the greater part of the northern temperate zone, it includes every variety of climate, from the hot unhealthy swamps of Florida, to the cold mountainous regions of northern New England, and the north-western territories.

6. The soil and productions of our country are as various as its climate. Compared with other countries, it contains a large proportion of arable land; and what is of the utmost consequence to the accommodation of man, it is *well watered.* On the whole, it may be pronounced, one of the most fertile, healthy, and desirable regions of the earth.

Side notes: CHAP. I. Connected with its geography and chronology. Where our country is. Its latitude and longitude. Its climate. Soil. Natural advantages.

3. Their geography? Are chronology and geography connected with history?—4. In regard to the universe where, as astronomy teaches, are the United States? In regard to the earth's surface, as respects geography, where is this country? What can you say of its extent?—5. What of its longitude? Of its latitude? Climate?—6. Soil and productions? Its natural advantages generally?—7. Does this region seem designed for one great nation, or for several small ones?

Suppose that a special machine transported you 100 years into the future. What might a textbook from that year look like? Why do you think that history textbooks change over time?

Source: Adapted from Emma Willard, *Abridged History of the United States, or Republic of America.* New York and Chicago: A. S. Barnes & Company, 1869.

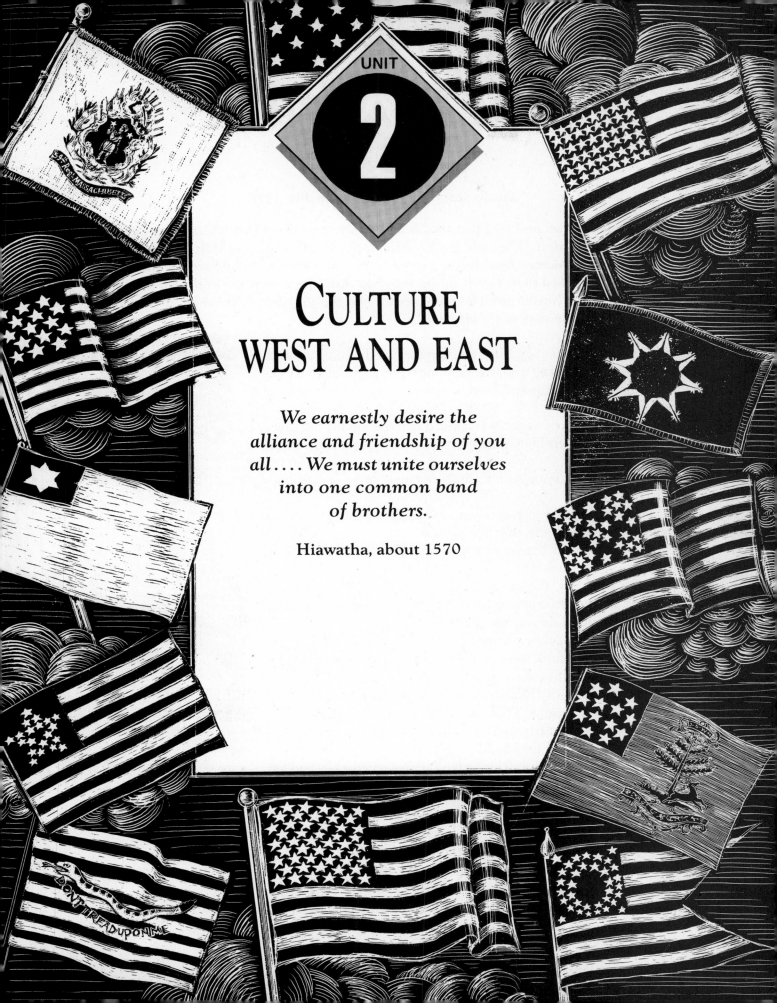

CULTURE WEST AND EAST

We earnestly desire the alliance and friendship of you all.... We must unite ourselves into one common band of brothers.

Hiawatha, about 1570

THE BEAUTIFUL DREAM

Navajo Story Told by Lana Semallie, 1976

The Navajo have an oral tradition that helps them to pass down their culture from one generation to the next. They told their stories, legends, and history to their children. In 1976 a writer named Byrd Baylor visited Native American schoolchildren in the Southwest and asked them to tell stories they had heard from someone in their tribes. Lana Semallie, a Navajo girl living in Arizona, told the story below. In which ways do the animals in this story act like people?

Many centuries ago Maii, the Coyote, was hanging around.

Coyote always liked to plan something tricky so this day he went walking with Porcupine and Brother Skunk. He was thinking as he walked along.

Ahead of them a wagon was going down the road. They saw a piece of meat fall off. They all ran for it and they all got there about the same time.

But Coyote did not want to share the meat so he said, "That's not fair."

He suggested they all race down a hill and the winner would eat the meat by himself. So that is what they did.

The race started. Porcupine curled up and rolled down the hill. He won.

"That's not fair," Coyote said.

Coyote suggested another plan. He said, "The one who dreams the most beautiful dream will eat that meat."

So that is what they planned.

Coyote and Skunk went to sleep but Porcupine stayed awake. He had a plan of his own.

Finally Coyote and Skunk woke up and told their dreams. They were both good dreams. They were both beautiful dreams.

Then they asked Porcupine what he had dreamed.

Porcupine said, "I dreamed I ate the meat."

They all jumped up and looked in the tree where they had left the meat. The meat was gone and Porcupine was looking fat.

Coyote is a popular character who appears over and over again in stories of the Navajo and other Southwest Indians. He is usually a funny character who gets into mischief when trying to trick his friends. But no matter how clever Coyote is, he often ends up getting fooled. If you were to write a story about Coyote, what adventures would you make up? What kinds of mischief would you have him getting into?

Source: Byrd Baylor, *And It Is Still That Way*. New York: Charles Scribner's Sons, 1976.

Aztec Poetry from Nahuatl Texts

Retold by Toni de Gerez, 1971

The Aztec civilization dates back to ancient times in what we now call Mexico. By the fifteenth century, the Aztec had conquered many other peoples and created a mighty empire. The Aztec poem below celebrates and mourns the passing of Quetzalcoatl (ket sahl KWAH tul), who was both an Aztec god and an historical person. The real-life Quetzalcoatl lived in the A.D. 900s. He was a priest-king of Tollan, an Aztec city also known as Tula. Quetzalcoatl brought the arts of writing, drawing, metal-working, and pottery-making to the Aztec. He also abolished human sacrifice. The Aztec god Quetzalcoatl was believed to be the god of learning and agriculture. Perhaps the historical and the religious figures are merged in this Aztec poem. Which aspects of Quetzalcoatl seem most important to the speaker of the poem?

Where is the house of **quetzal**
    feathers?
where is the house of turquoise?
where is the house of shells?

in Tollan
in Tollan
    o ay!

but our lord Quetzalcoatl has
    vanished
he has gone to **Tlapallan**
to the red-and-black country
    o ay!

In Tollan they say
there were birds rare and
    beautiful
small birds the color of
    turquoise
birds with green-and-yellow
    feathers
and yellow birds with breasts
    fire-color
    flame-color
and all sang in the name of our
    prince
o **Nactitl**
    o ay!
    o ay!

In Tollan squashes
were round and heavy as drums
    and gold as morning

an ear of corn
was as big as the great tongue
of the **metlatl**
    the yellow corn
    the red corn
    the dark corn
and one ear was all a man could
    carry

amaranth leaves were as big
    as palm fronds
you could climb up on them

and cotton grew on the bushes
in balls of every color
blue and green and red and
    yellow

in Tollan
in Tollan
    o ay!
    o ay!
our lord Quetzalcoatl has
    vanished

quetzal: Central American bird

Tlapallan: historic Aztec city

Nactitl: legendary king of Tollan

metlatl: the stone on which corn and chocolate are ground

amaranth: group of weeds and garden plants grown for their colorful leaves and flowers

Scholars and translators of Aztec poetry say that each poem must be seen as a part of one long poem. Together, they form a large body of literature that tells us what was vital to the Aztec culture. They were also used in religious dances and ceremonies.

Source: Toni de Gerez, *2-Rabbit, 7-Wind: Poems from Ancient Mexico Retold from Nahuatl Texts*. New York: Viking Press, 1971.

A Lakota Winter Count

by Lone Dog, 1801–1870

How do you keep track of past events that have happened in your life? Do you use a calendar or perhaps keep a diary? For hundreds of years, the Lakota Sioux used a special kind of calendar to keep track of their history. These calendars were called winter counts because each winter the Lakota chose an important event of the past year. An artist then recorded this event by drawing a pictograph, or picture, on the hide of an animal.

During the 1800s a Lakota named Lone Dog, who lived in what is today Montana, recorded in red and black on a buffalo hide most of the winter count shown on the next page. The first pictograph in Lone Dog's winter count dates from the winter of 1800-1801. This pictograph, which is highlighted, shows three short columns of 30 parallel lines. These lines stand for the deaths of 30 Lakota who were killed in battle during the past year. You can read each year of the winter count by following the pictographs in a spiral, counter-clockwise. Lone Dog wrote the final pictograph in the winter of 1869-1870.

Here is another example of a pictograph and the story it tells:

1840-1841. Two hands are about to grasp each other. This shaking of hands stood for a peace agreement between the Lakota and the Cheyenne. The hands are different colors to represent two different peoples.

Locate this pictograph in the winter count on the next page. Then study Lone Dog's other pictographs. See if you can figure out their meanings before checking the key on page 14, which explains some of them. How does the winter count show the events and issues that the Lakota considered important? How is Lone Dog a historian of his people?

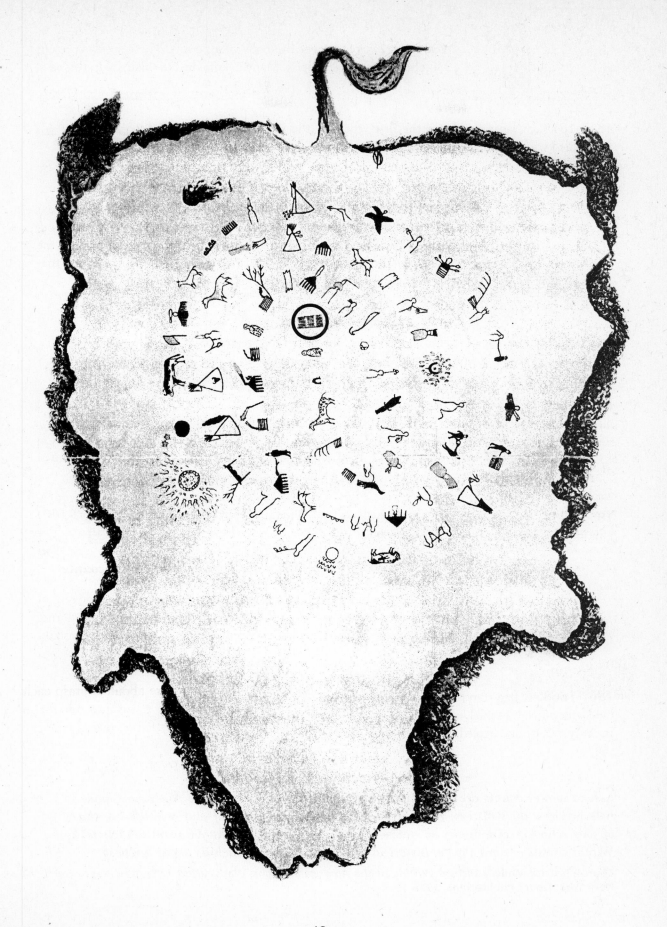

1801-1802. Spots cover the body of a person. These spots represent blotches caused by smallpox. Many Lakota died of smallpox in this year.

1812-1813. A lasso stands for the first year that the Lakota caught and tamed wild horses.

1817-1818. A building with smoke coming out of its chimney is next to a dead tree, which means that the structure was built with dry wood. During this year a Canadian trader built a store near the Lakota in the valley of the Minnesota River. Can you find other pictographs that show trading stores or forts?

1825-1826. Five circles appear above a line. The circles may represent the heads of people trying to stay above water. The Missouri River overflowed its banks in 1825 and caused a major flood, killing many Lakota.

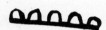

1833-1834. The moon is surrounded by many falling stars. On November 12, 1833, a great meteor shower fell all over the United States.

1853-1854. A man wearing a hat holds out a striped blanket. The Lakota exchanged many goods with traders this year.

1861-1862. Buffalo tracks appear beside a tepee. Note the cloven, or split, hoofs, characteristic of the buffalo. Food was so plentiful during this year that buffalo seemed to come right up to the Lakota's homes.

1867-1868. A flag stands for a peace conference that Lakota leaders held with officials of the United States government. The two groups met in August 1867 and agreed to a peace treaty during the following year.

Lakota winter counts are one of many written documents that Native Americans made to help preserve their history. If you were to make a winter count of your own life—or that of your school or community or state—what kinds of events might you want to include? Winter counts are one type of historical document that can teach us about the past.

Source: Garrick Mallery, *Picture-Writing of the American Indians*. Washington, D.C., 1893; reprinted New York: Dover Publications, 1972

Founding of the Iroquois League

by Hiawatha, about 1570

During the 1500s five Native American peoples known as the Iroquois were living in what is today New York State. These five peoples—the Onondaga, the Oneida, the Seneca, the Cayuga, and the Mohawk—fought frequently with each other. Around 1570, however, a Mohawk chief named Hiawatha began to spread a message of peace among the Iroquois. In one powerful speech he urged the five peoples to stop fighting and unite into a peaceful league, or union. Hiawatha's words were passed down by Iroquois families for hundreds of years, a tradition known as oral history. Then, in 1881, an Iroquois chief named Elias Johnson wrote an English version of the speech as it had been told to him. This is the version of Hiawatha's speech that you are about to read. Note the different terms Hiawatha uses to refer to the place where each people believed its creation began. These terms are printed in italics. How does Hiawatha describe the strength of each Iroquois people?

Friends and Brothers: You being members of many tribes, you have come from a great distance; the voice of war has aroused you up; you are afraid . . . [for] your homes, your wives and your children; you tremble for your safety. Believe me, I am with you. My heart beats with your hearts. We are one. We have one common object. We come to promote our common interest, and to determine how this can be best done.

To oppose those **hordes** of northern tribes, singly and alone, would prove certain destruction. We can make no progress in that way. We must unite ourselves into one common band of brothers. We must have but one voice. Many voices makes confusion. We must have one fire, one pipe [of peace] and one war club. This will give us strength. If our warriors are united they can defeat the enemy and drive them from our land; if we do this, we are safe.

hordes: crowds

Onondaga, you are the people sitting under the shadow of the *Great Tree*, whose branches spread far and wide, and whose roots sink deep into the earth. You shall be the first nation, because you are warlike and mighty.

Oneida, and you, the people who recline your bodies against the *Everlasting Stone*, that cannot be moved, shall be the second nation, because you always give good **counsel**.

Seneca, and you, the people who have your **habitation** at the foot of the *Great Mountain*, and are overshadowed by its **crags**, shall be the third nation, because you are all greatly gifted in speech.

Cayuga, you, whose dwelling is in the *Dark Forest*, and whose home is everywhere, shall be the fourth nation, because of your superior cunning in hunting.

Mohawk, and you, the people who live in the open country, and possess much wisdom, shall be the fifth nation, because you understand better the art of raising corn and beans and making cabins.

Great Tree: tree of peace, or white pine

Everlasting Stone: rock near present-day Oneida, New York

counsel: advice

habitation: home

Great Mountain: hill near Canandaigua Lake

crags: steep cliffs

Dark Forest: forest near Cayuga Lake

You five great and powerful nations, with your tribes, must unite and have one common interest, and no **foe** shall disturb or **subdue** you.

foe: enemy

subdue: conquer

And you of the different nations of the south, and you of the west, may place yourselves under our protection, and we will protect you. We earnestly desire the **alliance** and friendship of you all. . . .

alliance: cooperation

If we unite in one band the Great Spirit will smile upon us, and we shall be free, prosperous and happy; but if we shall remain as we are we shall **incur** his displeasure. We shall be enslaved, and perhaps **annihilated** forever.

incur: bring on

annihilated: destroyed

Brothers, these are the words of Hiawatha. Let them sink deep into your hearts. I have done.

Hiawatha's speech helped convince his listeners to put aside their differences and unite. Leaders of the five peoples formed a new government and called themselves the Iroquois League. A sixth people, the Tuscarora, joined the league in 1712. The Iroquois soon became one of the most powerful Native American groups in North America. Benjamin Franklin, a leader in the fight for American freedom from Great Britain in the 1700s, admired the league's strength and system of government. He later urged people in the 13 colonies to consider a similar plan of union.

Source: Elias Johnson (A Native Tuscarora Chief), *Legends, Traditions and Laws, of the Iroquois, or Six Nations, and History of the Tuscarora Indians.* Lockport, NY: Union Printing and Publishing Co., 1881.

HOW RAVEN MADE THE TIDES

Tsimshian Legend Told by Joseph Bruchac, 1991

Having respect for all living things on Earth is important to most Native American peoples. Regarding animals as their brothers and sisters, Native Americans often use them as characters in their stories. Raven is a favorite character in the stories of Native Americans from the Northwest Coast. Although he sometimes uses magic, Raven also uses clever tricks to achieve his goals. His actions often change the lives of people in important ways. In "How Raven Made the Tides," clever Raven outwits the old woman who has held back the ocean's tides. According to this legend, how did Raven's actions help the Native Americans of the Northwest Coast?

A long time ago, the old people say, the tide did not come in or go out.

The ocean would stay very high up on the shore for a long time and the clams and the seaweed and the other good things to eat would be hidden under the deep water. The people were often hungry.

"This is not the way it should be," said Raven. Then he put on his blanket of black feathers and flew along the coast, following the line of the tide. At last he came to the house of a very old woman who was the one who held the **tide-line** in her hand. As long as she held onto it the tide would stay high. Raven walked into the old

tide-line: furthest reach inland of the tide

17

woman's house. There she sat, the tide-line held firmly in her hand. Raven sat down across from her.

"Ah," he said, "those clams were good to eat."

"What clams?" said the old woman.

But Raven did not answer her. Instead he patted his stomach and said, "Ah, it was so easy to pick them up that I have eaten as much as I can eat."

"That can't be so," said the old woman, trying to look past Raven to see out her door, but Raven blocked the entrance. So she stood up and leaned past him to look out. Then Raven pushed her so that she fell through the door, and as she fell he threw dust into her eyes so that she was blinded. She let go of the tide-line then and the tide rushed out, leaving all kinds of clams and crabs and other good things to eat exposed.

Raven went out and began to gather clams. He gathered as much as he could carry and ate until he could eat no more. All along the beach others were gathering the good food and thanking Raven for what he had done. Finally he came back to the place where the old woman still was. "Raven," she said, "I know it is you. Heal my eyes so that I can see again."

"I will heal you," Raven said, "but only if you promise to let go of the tide-line twice a day. The people cannot wait so long to gather food from the beaches."

"I will do it," said the old woman. Then Raven washed out her eyes and she could see again. So it is that the tide comes in and goes out every day because Raven made the old woman let go of the tide-line.

The stories told by Native Americans are often more complicated than, for instance, the animal fables of Aesop. Native American tales can usually be interpreted in more than one way. Although the stories are intended as lessons, listeners of different ages find different meanings in them. What are several varying ways you might describe the character and actions of Raven?

Source: Joseph Bruchac, *Native American Stories.* Golden, CO: Fulcrum Publishing, 1991.

Yeh-hsien

Chinese Folk Tale Retold by Judy Sierra, 1992

Did you know that many of the folk tales we read today were first told thousands of years ago? From China, one of Earth's oldest civilizations, comes the first full version of the Cinderella story to be written down. The tale of Yeh-hsien (YE shen) was originally passed on from one storyteller to the next, in the oral tradition. This tradition preserved a body of literature until it could be written down. It may surprise you to learn that there are several hundred versions of the Cinderella story. While each culture tells the story somewhat differently, the core of the tale is always the same. A poor but good child is mistreated by a cruel family. She is aided by a magical being and is at last rewarded by a prosperous marriage and happiness. The voyages of Zheng He (ZHAHNG huh), a fifteenth-century Chinese explorer, helped to bring new stories to and from China and its neighboring countries. How might you expect the tale of Yeh-hsien to differ from the Cinderella story you know?

Among the people of the south there is a tradition that before the **Ch'in and Han dynasties** there lived a **cave-master** called Wu. People called the place the Wu cave. He had two wives. One wife died. She had a daughter called Yeh-hsien, who from childhood was intelligent and good at making pottery on the wheel. Her father loved her. After some years the father died, and she was ill-treated by her stepmother, who would always order her to collect firewood in dangerous places and draw water from deep pools. Once Yeh-hsien caught a fish about two inches long, with red fins and golden eyes. She put it into a bowl of water. It grew bigger every day, and after she had changed the bowl several times, she could find no bowl big enough for it, so she threw it back into the pond. Whatever food was left over from meals she put into the water to feed it. When Yeh-hsien came to the pond, the fish always swam up and rested its head on the bank, but when anyone else came, it would not come out.

The stepmother watched for the fish, but it did not once appear. So she tricked the girl, saying, "Haven't you worked hard! I am going to give you a new dress." She then made the girl change out of her tattered clothing. Afterwards she sent her to get water from a spring that was very far away. The stepmother put on Yeh-hsien's clothes, hid a sharp knife up her sleeve, and went to the pond. She called to the fish. The fish at once put its head out, and she chopped it off and killed it. The fish was now more than ten feet long. She cooked it, and when she served it up, it tasted twice as good as an ordinary fish. She hid the bones under the dung-hill.

The next day, when the girl came to the pond, no fish appeared. The girl ran out into the fields, howling with grief. Suddenly there appeared a man with his hair loose over his shoulders, dressed in

Ch'in and Han dynasties: ruling families of China from 226 B.C. to A.D. 220

cave-master: wise man who lived in a cave

coarse clothes. He descended from the sky, and he consoled her, saying, "Don't cry so! Your stepmother has killed the fish and its bones are under the dung-heap. Go back, take the fish's bones and hide them in your room. Whatever you want, you have only to ask the fish bones for it." The girl followed his advice, and from then on she was able to provide herself with gold, pearls, dresses, and food whenever she wanted them.

When the time came for the cave festival, the stepmother took her own daughter with her, and left Yeh-hsien to keep watch over the fruit trees in the garden. The girl waited until they were far away, and then she followed them, wearing a cloak of material spun from **kingfisher** feathers and shoes of gold. Her stepsister saw her and said to the stepmother, "That girl looks like my sister." The stepmother suspected the same thing. The girl was aware of this and went away in such a hurry that she lost one shoe. It was picked up by one of the people of the cave. When the stepmother got home, she found the girl asleep, with her arms round one of the trees in the garden, and thought no more about it.

kingfisher: bright-colored bird that eats fish

The cave was near an island in the sea, and on this island was a kingdom called T'o-han. The man who had picked up the gold shoe sold it in T'o-han, and it was brought to the king. He ordered all the women of the court to put it on, but it was too small even for the one among them that had the smallest foot. He then ordered all the women in his kingdom to try it on, but there was not one that it fitted. It was as light as **down**, and it made no noise even when treading on stone. His search finally took him to the place where Yeh-hsien lived with her stepmother, and the shoe fitted her perfectly. She put on the other shoe, and her cape of feathers, and she was as beautiful as a heavenly being. Taking the fish bones with her, she returned with the king to T'o-han and became his chief wife. The first year, the king was very greedy and asked the fish bones for **jade** and pearls without limit. The next year, the fish bones no longer granted his requests. He buried them by the sea shore and covered them with a hundred **bushels** of pearls, and after a while they were washed away by the tide.

down: soft feathers

jade: very hard, green mineral used for jewelry

bushel: unit of measure equal to 32 quarts

The stepmother and stepsister were struck by flying rocks, and died. The cave people buried them in a stone pit, which was called the Tomb of the Two Women. Men would come there and make offerings, and the girl they prayed for would become their wife.

In the European version of the story that you probably know, Cinderella marries the prince, who is as good and deserving as she is. How would you describe the character of the king in "Yeh-hsien"? How else are the European and Chinese versions alike or different?

Source: Judy Sierra, *The Oryx Multicultural Folktale Series: Cinderella.* Phoenix: Oryx Press, 1992.

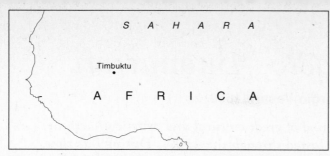

Timbuktu

by Leo Africanus, 1526

During the 1400s Songhai (SAWNG hǐ) was one of the largest kingdoms in West Africa. Timbuktu was one of the major centers of trade in Songhai and a great cultural center. Trade brought great wealth to the kingdom and to the city. It was said that in Timbuktu books were "sold for more money than any other merchandise." Why do you think books were so valued? The following description of Timbuktu is from a history of North Africa by an Arab scholar called Leo Africanus, written in the 1500s.

Timbuktu is situated within twelve miles of a certain branch of [the] **Niger**, all the houses **whereof** are now changed into cottages built of chalk, and covered with thatch. **How be it** there is a most stately temple to be seen, the walls **thereof** are made of stone and lime; and a princely palace also built by a most excellent workman of **Granada**. Here are many shops of **artificers**, and merchants, and especially of such as weave linen and cotton cloth. And **hither** do the **Barbary** merchants bring cloth of Europe....Corn, cattle, milk and butter this region **yieldeth** in great abundance; but salt is very scarce here; for it is brought hither by land from Tegaza, which is five hundred miles distant....

The rich king of Timbuktu hath many plates and **scepters** of gold, some whereof weigh 1,300 pounds: and he keeps a magnificent and well furnished court....He hath always three thousand horsemen, and a great number of footmen that shoot poisoned arrows, attending upon him. They have often skirmishes with those that refuse to pay tribute....Here are great store of doctors, judges, priests, and other learned men, that are bountifully maintained at the king's cost and charges. And hither are brought diverse manuscripts or written books out of Barbary which are sold for more money than any other merchandise. The coin of Timbuktu is of gold without any stamp or superscription; but in matters of small value they use certain shells brought hither out of the kingdom of Persia, four hundred of which shells are worth a **ducat**....The inhabitants are people of a gentle and cheerful **disposition**, and spend a great part of the night in singing and dancing through all the streets of the city: they keep great store of men and women-slaves, and their town is much in danger of fire: at my second being there half the town almost was burnt in five hours space. Without the suburbs there are no gardens or orchards at all.

Niger: river in West Africa
whereof: there
How be it: Nonetheless
thereof: of which
Granada: Islamic kingdom in Spain at that time
artificers: craftspeople
hither: here
Barbary: North Africa
yieldeth: gives
scepters: staffs or rods held by a king

ducat: type of money
disposition: way of being

Scholars from all over the world came to Timbuktu to study at its university, and the kingdom of Songhai saw many travelers and explorers from Europe seeking gold, ivory, and other riches.

Source: Adapted from Robin Hallett, *The Penetration of Africa*. New York: Frederick A. Praeger, Inc., 1965.

Michelangelo Buonarroti

by Giorgio Vasari, 1550

The Renaissance (ren uh SAHNS), a period of great cultural and artistic growth in Europe, began in Italy in the 1300s and lasted through the 1500s. During this time, people became interested in broadening their horizons and in learning about ideas that were new to them. Many artists, such as Michelangelo Buonarroti (mi kuh LAN juh loh BUO nuh ROH tee, 1475-1563) produced magnificent works of art. The following excerpt is from a book of short biographies by a friend of Michelangelo's who was also an artist. The biographer describes how Michelangelo created the paintings on the ceiling of the Sistine Chapel in Rome, which are considered to be among the finest artwork of all time. What personal qualities helped Michelangelo produce such great work?

The **master** accordingly finished the whole, completing it to perfection in twenty months, without having even the help of a man to **grind the colours**. It is true that he sometimes complained of the manner in which the **Pope** hastened forward the work, seeing that he was thereby prevented from giving it the finish which he would have desired to bestow; His Holiness constantly inquiring when it would be completed. On one occasion, therefore, Michelangelo replied, "It will be finished when I shall have done all that I believe required to satisfy Art." "And we command," rejoined the Pontiff, "that you satisfy our wish to have it done quickly"; adding finally, that if it were not at once completed, he would have him, Michelangelo, thrown headlong from the scaffolding.

...He worked with great inconvenience to himself, having to labour with the face turned upwards, and injuring his eyes so much in the progress of the work, that he could neither read letters nor examine drawings for several months afterwards....

Michelangelo found his chief pleasure in the labours of art.... For the greater **exactitude**, he made numerous **dissections** of the human frame, examining the anatomy of each part.... These labours enabled him to complete his works, whether of the pencil or chisel, with perfection, and to give them a grace, a beauty, and an animation, **wherein**...he has surpassed even **the antique**....

His powers of imagination were such that he was frequently compelled to abandon his purpose, because he could not express by the hand those grand and sublime ideas which he had conceived in his mind, nay, he has spoiled and destroyed many works for this cause; and I know too that some short time before his death he burnt a large number of his designs and sketches...that none might see the labours he had endured in his resolve not to fall short of perfection.

The master: honorary term for a great artist; here applied to Michelangelo

grind the colours: make the paints

Pope: Julius II

exactitude: accuracy

dissections: examinations

wherein: where

the antique: the artists of "antiquity," or the Greek and Roman times

New knowledge and inventions discovered during the Renaissance enabled men such as Henry the Navigator to search for a shorter, cheaper route to Asia. Later, Columbus, seeking this same route to the silk and spices of the East, reached the Americas and changed the course of history.

Source: James Hanscom, Leon Hellerman, and Ronald Posner, eds., *Voices of the Past: Readings in Medieval and Early Modern History.* New York: The Macmillan Company, 1967.

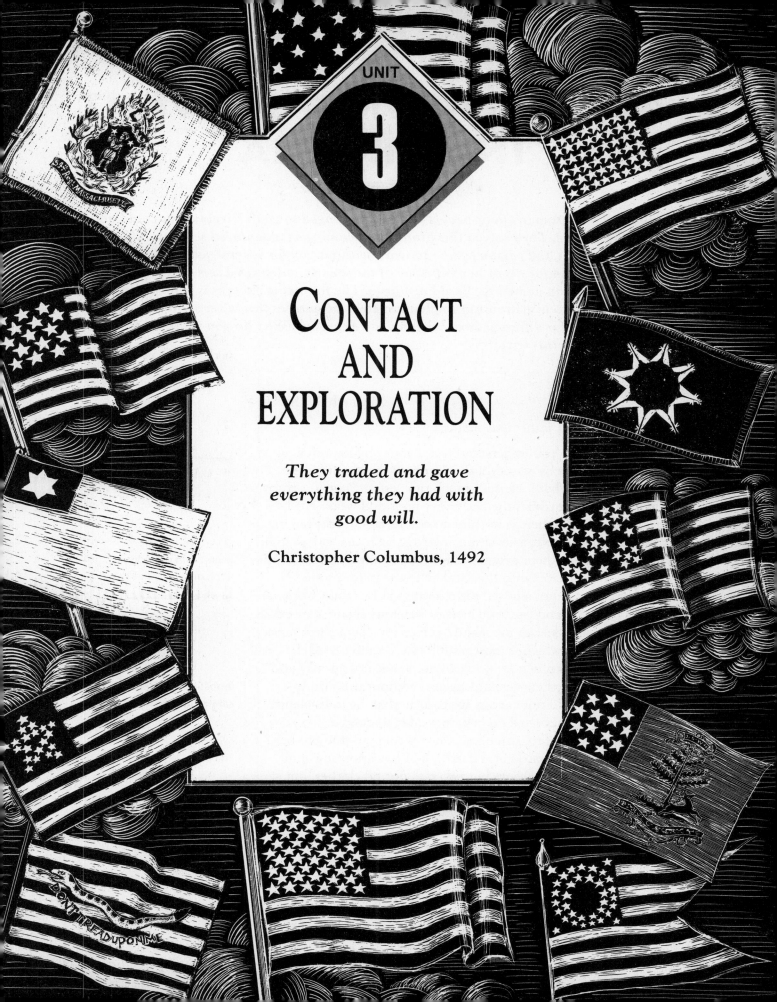

CONTACT AND EXPLORATION

They traded and gave everything they had with good will.

Christopher Columbus, 1492

AN INDENTURED SERVANT IN VIRGINIA

by Richard Frethorne, 1623

In the early 1600s many poor people in England longed to go to Virginia but could not afford the voyage. They solved this problem by coming as indentured servants. Under this arrangement, the person agreed to work without pay for several years for a colonist who paid for his or her trip. One of these early indentured servants was a young Englishman named Richard Frethorne. The following excerpt is from a letter he wrote home to his parents in England in 1623. How does this letter show that life in Virginia was far different from what he had expected? Why do you think that Frethorne wrote this letter?

[March 20, 1623]

Loving and kind father and mother:

This is to let you understand that I your child am in a most **heavy case** by reason of the nature of the country, [which] is such that it causeth much sickness . . . and . . . diseases, which maketh the body very poor and weak. And when we are sick there is nothing to comfort us; for since I came out of the ship, I never ate anything but peas and loblollie (that is, water **gruel**). As for deer or **venison** I never saw any since I came into this land. There is indeed some **fowl**, but we are not allowed to go and get it, but must work hard both early and late for a mess of water gruel and a mouthful of bread and beef. A mouthful of bread for a penny loaf must serve for 4 men which is most pitiful. [You would be sad] if you did know as much as I [do], when people cry out day and night—Oh, that they were in England without their **limbs**! And [they] would not **care to lose** any limb to be in England again [even if] they [had to] beg from door to door. . . .

I have nothing to comfort me, nor is there nothing to be gotten here but sickness and death. . . . I have nothing at all; no, not a shirt to my back, but two rags nor no clothes, but one poor suit, nor but one pair of shoes, but one pair of stockings, but one cap, [and] but two **bands**. My cloak is stolen by one of my own **fellows**, and to his dying hour [he] would not tell me what he did with it. But some of my fellows saw him have butter and beef out of a ship, which my cloak, I doubt [not] paid for, so that I have not a penny, nor a penny

heavy case: sad condition

gruel: thin porridge
venison: deer meat
fowl: birds

limbs: arms or legs
care to lose: mind losing

bands: belts
fellows: friends

worth to help me. . . . I am not half [of] a quarter so strong as I was in England, and all is for want of **victuals**, for I do protest unto you that I have eaten more in [one] day at home than I have . . . here for a week. . . .

victuals: food

I find [myself in] . . . great grief and misery, and [I] saith, that if you love me you will **redeem me** suddenly, for which I do **entreat** and beg. And if you cannot get the merchants to redeem me for some little money, then for God's sake . . . entreat some good folks to lay out some little sum of money, in **meal** and cheese and butter and beef. Any eating meat will yield great profit. . . . Good father, do not forget me, but have mercy and pity my miserable case. I know if you did but see me you would weep to see me, for I have but one suit. . . . For God's sake, pity me. I pray you to remember my love . . . to all my friends and **kindred**. I hope all my brothers and sisters are in good health, and as for my part I have set down my **resolution** that . . . the answer of this letter will be life or death to me. Therefore, good father, send as soon as you can. . . .

redeem me: buy back my period of service

entreat: plead

meal: grains

kindred: family

resolution: belief

Richard Frethorne

What became of Richard Frethorne remains a mystery. Whether he returned to England, stayed in Virginia, or died young is unknown. Life in Virginia remained full of hunger, hardships, and disease throughout the 1600s. Still, indentured servants continued to pour into the colony in hopes of a better life. Many completed the long period of service and gained their freedom. Not only whites were indentured servants. Most of the first Africans in Virginia—although brought by force to America—were treated like indentured servants in the early and middle 1600s. Many of these Africans also gained their freedom. Altogether, more than half of the people who came to Virginia between 1607 and 1776 came, like Richard Frethorne, as indentured servants.

Source: Adapted from Susan Myra Kingsbury, ed., *The Records of the Virginia Company of London*, Vol. IV. Washington, D.C.: Government Printing Office, 1935.

The Mayflower Compact

Pilgrim Agreement, 1620

When the passengers aboard the Mayflower saw that they had reached New England instead of Virginia in 1620, they quickly realized that their new home was not subject to any European laws. How would this new colony govern itself? To answer this question, Pilgrim leaders drew up a compact, or agreement, and 41 of the ship's 101 passengers signed it before they went ashore. As you read the Mayflower Compact below and the rewritten modern version on the next page, think about what the signers are agreeing to do. Why do they believe it is important to set up a government? Note the names of the people who signed the compact. Why do you think there are no women's names?

In the Name of God, Amen. We, whose names are underwritten, the Loyal Subjects of our dread Sovereign Lord King *James*, by the Grace of God, of *Great Britain, France,* and *Ireland*, King, *Defender of the Faith*, etc. Having undertaken for the Glory of God, and Advancement of the Christian Faith, and the Honour of our King and Country, a Voyage to plant the first Colony in the northern Parts of *Virginia*; Do by these Presents, solemnly and mutually, in the Presence of God and one another, covenant and combine ourselves together into a civil Body Politick, for our better Ordering and Preservation, and Furtherance of the Ends aforesaid; And by Virtue hereof do enact, constitute, and frame, such just and equal Laws, Ordinances, Acts, Constitutions, and Officers, from time to time, as shall be thought most meet and convenient for the general Good of the Colony; unto which we promise all due Submission and Obedience. IN WITNESS whereof we have hereunto subscribed our names at *Cape-Cod* the eleventh of *November*, in the Reign of our Sovereign Lord King *James*, of *England, France,* and *Ireland*, the eighteenth, and of *Scotland*, the fifty-fourth, *Anno Domini*, 1620.

Mr. John Carver	Mr. Samuel Fuller	Edward Tilly
Mr. William Bradford	Mr. Christopher Martin	John Tilly
Mr. Edward Winslow	Mr. William Mullins	Francis Cooke
Mr. William Brewster	Mr. William White	Thomas Rogers
Isaac Allerton	Mr. Richard Warren	Thomas Tinker
Miles Standish	John Howland	John Ridgale
John Alden	Mr. Steven Hopkins	Edward Fuller
John Turner	Digery Priest	Richard Clark
Francis Eaton	Thomas Williams	Richard Gardiner
James Chilton	Gilbert Winslow	Mr. John Allerton
John Craxton	Edmund Margesson	Thomas English
John Billington	Peter Brown	Edward Doten
Joses Fletcher	Richard Bitteridge	Edward Liester
John Goodman	George Soule	

In the name of God, Amen. We, who have signed our names below, are the loyal subjects of King James of Great Britain. In honor of God, our Christian religion, our king, and our country, we took a voyage to build the first colony in northern Virginia. To keep order in this colony, we agree in this document to join together under one government. We promise to make laws and rules that are fair and will apply equally to everyone. We also promise to obey these laws and rules. We hope that the laws, rules, and leaders we choose will both improve and help preserve the colony.

Having read and agreed to this compact, we have signed our names at Cape Cod on November 11, 1620.

In addition to helping Plymouth colony grow, the Mayflower Compact helped to establish the idea of self-government among European colonists in North America. Over 150 years later this idea would be clearly expressed in another important document—the Declaration of Independence. You can read this document on pages 62–66.

Source: Ben. Perley Poore, *The Federal and State Constitutions*, Part 1. New York: Burt Franklin, 1924.

Reaching the Americas

by Christopher Columbus, 1492

On August 3, 1492, Christopher Columbus (1451–1506) and his crew of 90 sailors set sail from Spain on three ships hoping to find a new route to Asia. After stopping to get supplies in the Canary Islands, the crew sailed west across the Atlantic Ocean—a voyage no European had attempted in hundreds of years. What was this historic voyage like? Fortunately, Columbus kept a journal, or diary, of his trip. In the part of his journal you are about to read, Columbus describes the long, dangerous journey and the first sight of land, a small island in the Caribbean Sea. Notice Columbus's opinion of the Taino, the first people he meets in the Americas, and how the Taino treat the Europeans. In what ways does Columbus consider himself a trader and explorer? In what ways does he see himself as a conqueror as well?

September 9

This day we completely lost sight of land, and many men sighed and wept for fear they would not see it again for a long time. I comforted them with great promises of lands and riches. To **sustain** their hope and **dispel** their fears of a long voyage, I decided to **reckon** fewer **leagues** than we actually made. I did this that they might not think themselves so great a distance from Spain as they really were.

For myself I will keep a **confidential** accurate reckoning.

sustain: keep up
dispel: drive away
reckon: count
leagues: units of distance

confidential: secret

September 24

I am having serious trouble with the crew. . . . All day long and all night long those who are awake and able to get together never **cease** to talk to each other [as they gather] in circles, complaining that they will never be able to return home. They have said that it is insanity and **suicidal** on their part to risk their lives following the madness of a **foreigner**. . . . I am told by a few trusted men (and these are few in number!) that if I **persist** in going onward, the best course of action will be to throw me into the sea some night.

cease: stop

suicidal: very dangerous

foreigner: Columbus is called a foreigner because he was born in Italy

persist: continue

October 10

Between day and night I made 177 miles [285 km]. I told the crew 132 miles [212 km], but they could stand it no longer. They grumbled and complained of the long voyage, and I **reproached** them for their lack of spirit, telling them that, for better or worse, they had to complete the **enterprise** on which the **Catholic Sovereigns** had sent them.

reproached: scolded

enterprise: task

Catholic Sovereigns: Queen Isabella and King Ferdinand

October 11

About 10 o'clock at night, while standing on the **sterncastle**, I thought I saw a light to the west. It looked like a little wax candle bobbing up and down. It had the same appearance as a light or torch belonging to fishermen or travelers who **alternately** raised and lowered it, or perhaps were going from house to house. . . .

The moon, in its third quarter, rose in the east shortly before midnight. . . . Then, at two hours after midnight, the *Pinta* fired a cannon, my **prearranged** signal for the sighting of land.

I now believe that the light I saw earlier was a sign from God and that it was truly the first positive **indication** of land. When we caught up with the *Pinta*, which was always running ahead because she was a swift sailor, I learned that the first man to sight land was Rodrigo de Triana, a seaman from Lepe.

sterncastle: rear part of a boat

alternately: taking turns

prearranged: set up before

indication: sign

October 12

At dawn we saw . . . people, and I went ashore in the ship's boat, **armed**. . . . I **unfurled** the royal banner and the captains brought the flags which displayed a large green cross with the letters **F** and **Y** at the left and right side of the cross. . . .

No sooner had we concluded the **formalities** of taking possession of the island than people began to come to the beach. . . . All those that I saw were young people, none of whom was over 30 years old. They are very well-built people, with handsome bodies and very fine faces. . . . Their eyes are large and very pretty. . . . These are tall people and their legs, with no exceptions, are quite straight, and none of them has a **paunch**. They are, in fact, **well proportioned**. Their hair is . . . straight, and **coarse** like horsehair. They wear it short over the eyebrows, but they have a long **hank** in the back that they never cut. Many of the natives paint their faces; others paint their whole bodies; some, only the eyes or nose. Some are painted black, some white, some red; others are of different colors.

armed: carrying weapons
unfurled: unfolded
F: for Ferdinand
Y: for Ysabella, Isabella
formalities: ceremonies

paunch: big belly
well proportioned: well built
coarse: rough
hank: coil

The people here called this island *Guanahaní* in their language, and their speech is very **fluent**, although I do not understand any of it. They are friendly and **well-dispositioned** people who **bear no arms** except for small spears, and they have no iron. I showed one my sword, and through **ignorance** he grabbed it by the blade and cut himself. Their spears are made of wood, to which they attach a fish tooth at one end, or some other sharp thing. . . .

fluent: smooth and rapid

well-dispositioned: easygoing

bear no arms: carry no weapons

ignorance: not knowing

They traded and gave everything they had with good will, but it seems to me that they have very little and are poor in everything. . . .

This afternoon the people . . . came swimming to our ships and in boats made from one log. They brought us parrots, balls of cotton thread, spears, and many other things. . . . For these items we **swapped** them little glass beads and **hawks' bells**. . . .

swapped: traded

hawks' bells: small bells that attach to the leg of a hawk

They ought to make good and skilled servants, for they repeat very quickly whatever we say to them. . . . I will take six of them to Your Highnesses when I depart. . . .

October 13

After sunrise people . . . again began to come to our ships in boats **fashioned** in one piece from the trunks of trees. These boats are wonderfully made . . . and every bit as fine as those I have seen in **Guinea**. They come in all sizes. Some can carry 40 or 50 men; some are so small that only one man rides in it. . . .

fashioned: built

Guinea: region of western Africa

I have been very **attentive** and have tried very hard to find out if there is any gold here.

attentive: alert

Columbus left the Caribbean on January 15, 1493, with six Taino prisoners and arrived in Spain in March. News of his voyage spread quickly through Europe and changed the world forever. Columbus's journey had joined two "worlds"—the continents of North and South America and the continents of Europe, Asia, and Africa—that had been separated for thousands of years. European explorers, conquerors, and treasure hunters soon began streaming across the Atlantic Ocean in search of gold and other riches. Columbus returned to the Americas three more times. On his later voyages he enslaved thousands of Native Americans and forced them to dig for gold. The harsh treatment and diseases brought by European explorers soon caused the death of all the Taino. To learn about the Europeans' hunger for gold, read the next document on pages 31–32.

Source: Robert H. Fuson, translator, *The Log of Christopher Columbus*. Camden, ME: International Marine Publishing Company, 1987.

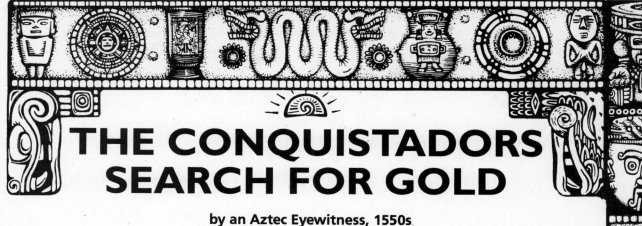

THE CONQUISTADORS SEARCH FOR GOLD

by an Aztec Eyewitness, 1550s

In the early 1500s Spanish conquerors, known as conquistadors, explored both North and South America. One of these conquistadors was 34-year-old Hernando Cortés. Like Christopher Columbus, whose journal you read on pages 28–30, Cortés hoped to find gold and other riches. In 1519 Cortés and about 500 Spanish soldiers marched through present-day Mexico and conquered one of the largest empires in the world—the Aztec empire. In the 1550s an historian interviewed an Aztec eyewitness who had seen the Spanish conquest. This witness described how Cortés and his men acted when they seized the fabulous treasures of the empire's capital city, Tenochtitlán. As you read this account, notice what the eyewitness sometimes compares the conquistadors to. Why do you suppose the eyewitness chose to make such comparisons?

When the Spaniards were **installed** in the palace, they asked **Motecuhzoma** about the city's resources and **reserves** and about the warriors' **ensigns** and shields. They questioned him closely and then demanded gold.

Motecuhzoma guided them to it. They surrounded him and crowded close with their weapons. He walked in the center, while they formed a circle around him.

When they arrived at the treasure house . . . the riches of gold and feathers were brought out to them: ornaments made of **quetzal** feathers, richly worked shields, disks of gold, the necklaces of the **idols**, . . . gold **greaves** and bracelets and crowns. . . .

The Spaniards burst into smiles; [and] their eyes shone with pleasure; they were delighted by them. They picked up the gold and fingered it like monkeys; they seemed to be **transported** by joy, as if their hearts were **illumined** and made new.

The truth is that they longed and **lusted for** gold. Their bodies swelled with greed, and their hunger was **ravenous**; they hungered like pigs for that gold. They snatched at the golden ensigns, waved them from side to side and examined every inch of them. . . .

The Spaniards immediately stripped the feathers from the gold shields and ensigns. They gathered all the gold into a great mound and set fire to everything else, regardless of its value. Then they

installed: settled
Motecuhzoma (maw tay kway SOH mah): Aztec emperor, also called Moctezuma and Montezuma
reserves: valuables

ensigns: flags

quetzal: a kind of bird

idols: statues of gods
greaves: leg armor

transported: carried away
illumined: lit up
lusted for: wanted strongly
ravenous: intense

melted down the gold into **ingots.** As for the precious green stones, they took only the best of them. . . .

ingots: bars

Next they went to Motecuhzoma's storehouse . . . where his personal treasures were kept. The Spaniards grinned like little beasts and patted each other with delight.

When they entered the hall of treasures, it was as if they had arrived in **Paradise.** They searched everywhere and **coveted** everything; they were slaves to their own greed. All of Motecuhzoma's possessions were brought out: fine bracelets, necklaces with large stones, ankle rings with little gold bells, the royal crowns and all the royal **finery**—everything that belonged to the king and was reserved to him only. They seized these treasures as if they were their own, as if this **plunder** were merely a stroke of good luck. And when they had taken all the gold, they heaped up everything else in th middle of the **patio.**

Paradise: heaven
coveted: wanted

finery: jewels and fancy clothing
plunder: stealing

patio: courtyard

By 1570, 50 years after the Spanish conquest, over 1 million Aztec had been killed by foreign diseases, warfare, and the effects of forced labor. By this time Cortés and other Spaniards had carried much of the Aztec gold back to Europe.

Source: Miguel Leon-Portilla, ed., *The Broken Spears: The Aztec Account of the Conquest of Mexico.* Boston: Beacon Press, 1962.

Drawings of Roanoke

by John White, 1585

The first English colonists who built a settlement on Roanoke Island (1585–1586) faced hunger and conflicts with the Native Americans who lived there, the Roanoac. The second group of colonists (1587–?) vanished, leaving a mystery that has not yet been solved by historians. All that is known for sure is that the colony had disappeared by the time colonial governor John White returned to the island in August 1590, bringing additional supplies. The Roanoke colony, although it failed, yielded enough information about the territory and climate of the region to enable later colonists to survive. John White's hand-drawn maps and other drawings show Roanoke and the surrounding land and waterways. Why do you think this area of the coast was so dangerous to vessels attempting to land?

The Algonquin village of Pomeiooc in what is now North Carolina was painted in watercolor by John White.

White's watercolor painting of Secoton, another Algonquin village in present-day North Carolina, includes cornfields and other details of daily life.

Sources: R. Conrad Stein, *America the Beautiful: North Carolina.* Chicago: Childrens Press, 1990; William S. Powell, *The North Carolina Colony.* London: Crowell-Collier Press, 1969; *Eugenia Burney, North Carolina.* New York: Thomas Nelson Inc., 1975.

This engraving, based on a lost drawing done by John White, shows the first group of English colonists arriving at Roanoke Island in 1585.

Governor John White used his artistry to draw and paint maps and pictures of the wildlife of Virginia and North Carolina. His work helped to spark European interest in North America. In 1607 Jamestown, Virginia was to become the first permanent English colony in North America. White also sketched Native American peoples of North Carolina, leaving a body of artwork that documents a whole way of life during the late 1500s.

John White's map of the Outer Banks of Virginia depicts Cape Lookout and Chesapeake Bay.

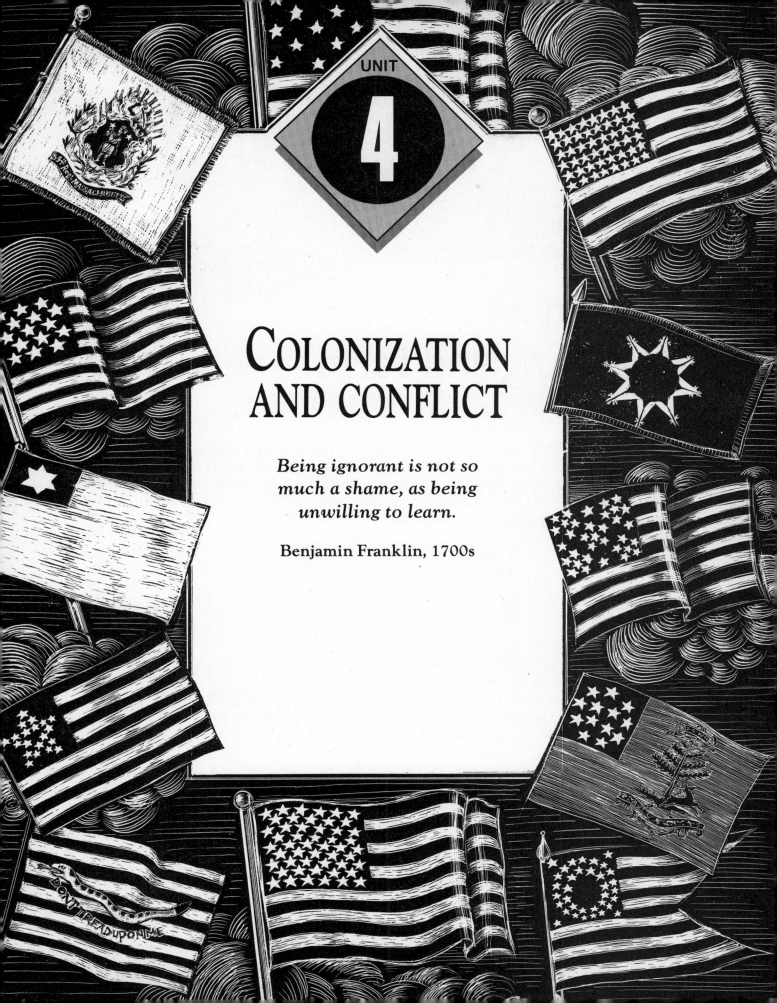

COLONIZATION AND CONFLICT

Being ignorant is not so much a shame, as being unwilling to learn.

Benjamin Franklin, 1700s

Life on a New England Farm

by Ruth Belknap, 1782

What was life like on a farm in colonial New England? For most people it meant hard work, especially for women. The following poem, written in 1782, gives an idea of some of the many chores performed by farm women. The poet, Ruth Belknap, was the wife of a minister and lived in Dover, New Hampshire. Why do you think she titled her poem "The Pleasures of a Country Life"?

The Pleasures of a Country Life

Up in the morning I must rise

Before I've time to rub my eyes.

With half-**pin'd** gown, unbuckled shoe,   **pin'd:** pinned

I haste to milk my **lowing** cow.   **lowing:** mooing

But, Oh! it makes my heart to ache,

I have no bread till I can bake,

And then, alas! it makes me sputter,

For I must **churn** or have no butter.   **churn:** stir milk into butter

The hogs with **swill** too I must serve;   **swill:** garbage fed to pigs

For hogs must eat or men will starve.

Besides, my **spouse** can get no clothes   **spouse:** mate; husband or wife

Unless I much offend my nose.

For all that try it know it's true

There is no smell like **coloring blue**.　　coloring blue: bleach

Then round the **parish** I must ride　　parish: area served by a minister

And **make enquiry** far and wide　　make enquiry: ask questions

To find some girl that is a **spinner**,　　spinner: person who makes yarn on a spinning wheel

Then hurry home to get my dinner. . . .

All summer long I toil & sweat,

Blister my hands, and scold & **fret**.　　fret: worry

And when the summer's work is **o'er**,　　o'er: over

New **toils** arise from Autumn's store.　　toils: jobs

Corn must be **husk'd**, and pork be kill'd,　　husk'd: stripped of its outer covering

The house with all confusion fill'd.

O could you see the grand display

Upon our annual butchering day. . . .　　parson: minister

Ye starch'd up folks that live in town,

That lounge upon your beds till noon,

That never tire yourselves with work,

Unless with handling knife & fork,

Come, see the sweets of country life,

Display'd in **Parson** B[elknap's] wife.

Although most women, like Ruth Belknap, worked on farms in colonial New England, many held other jobs as well. Some colonial women worked as printers, doctors, and merchants. Others ran inns and restaurants and owned their own businesses. For both women and men, there was never a lack of work in colonial New England.

Source: Laurel Thatcher Ulrich, *Good Wives: Image and Reality in the Lives of Women in Northern New England, 1650–1750*. New York: Oxford University Press, 1982.

A Pilgrim's Journal of Plymouth Plantation

by William Bradford, 1620

Europeans came to North America in the 1600s for many different reasons. The Pilgrims came in search of religious freedom and a life they thought would be better than the one they left behind in England. William Bradford (1590-1657) was one of the Pilgrims who came to what is now Massachusetts aboard the Mayflower. He later became governor of Plymouth, the new colony founded by the Pilgrims. Below is an entry from Bradford's journal. It was written shortly after the Pilgrims first reached North America. What did the Pilgrims find when they landed? Why were these discoveries so important to them?

December 18th. Monday, we went **a-land**, **manned with** the master of the ship and three or four of the sailors and marched along the coast in the woods some seven or eight miles. We found where **formerly** had been some inhabitants and where they had planted their corn, but saw not an Indian nor an Indian house. We found no **navigable** river but saw four or five small running brooks of very sweet fresh water that all run into the sea. **The crust of the earth is excellent black mold for a spit's depth**, and more in some places. There are two or three great oaks but not very thick, **pines, walnuts, beech, ash, birch, hazel, holly, asp, sassafras** in abundance, vines everywhere, cherry trees, plum trees, and many others which we know not.

Many kinds of herbs we found here in winter: strawberry leaves **innumerable**, sorrel, yarrow, chervil, brook-lime, liverwort, watercress, great store of leeks and onions, and an excellent strong kind of flax, and hemp. Here is sand, gravel, and excellent clay, no better in the world, excellent for pots and will wash like soap, and great store of stone, though somewhat soft. The best water that ever we drunk is here, and the streams now begin to be full of fish. That night, many of us being weary with marching, we went aboard again.

a-land: ashore
manned with: along with

formerly: previously

navigable: sailable by boats
The crust . . . a spit's depth: A spit holds meat while it's being roasted; Bradford is saying that the soil is rich and good for farming to a depth of perhaps two or three feet.
pines . . . sassafras: types of trees
innumerable: without number; that is, so many it's impossible to count them

The Pilgrims paved the way for other Europeans who came to North America during the 1600s and 1700s. These new groups built cities, towns, and farms. They established what is now the United States as a place where people from all over the world can seek a new and better life.

Source: William Bradford, et. al., "A Pilgrim's Journal of Plymouth Plantation in 1620" in *Homes in the Wilderness*, Margaret Wise Brown, ed. Hamden, CT: Linnet Books, 1988.

Penn's Woods

by Navidad O'Neill, 1996

In 1681, a Quaker named William Penn received a land grant from King Charles I to establish a colony in North America where Quakers could practice their religion freely. This play tells about the founding of this colony, which became the modern-day state of Pennsylvania. Besides religious freedom, what other ideals were important to Penn and his followers?

CAST OF CHARACTERS

William Penn, Quaker and founder of Pennsylvania
Charles, the king of England
Samantha, a colonist
Margaret, a colonist
Samuel, a colonist
Ben, a colonist
Sarah, a colonist

The playing area is divided into three sections: 1. The banks of a river in England; 2. The ship Welcome; 3. Philadelphia, Pennsylvania. The time is the late 1680s.

There is one important prop, the rolled-up document which King Charles II gives to William Penn, and which is later used as a banner reading "Welcome." A second rolled-up piece of paper is also needed for the Charter of Liberty.

King Charles and William Penn stand in a circle made by the colonists squatting down. Charles is writing on a document with a quill pen.

King: *(looking up at Penn)* What shall we call this land? We can't simply say, here, William Penn, take this 45,000 square miles in a rectangle shape, somewhere in America. Here, William Penn, govern this land about the size of England. Here, William Penn, for the debt I owe your father, instead of money take this piece of land. It needs a name, this broad rectangular land.

Penn: New Wales would be a good name for the new land, since it is mountainous like Wales in England.

King: No. No. Something else.

Penn: How about Sylvania, which means woods? I am told that the forests are magnificent in this new land across the sea.

King: I like that, but let's call it "Penn's woods." That is, "Pennsylvania."

Penn: You cannot name a land after me!

King: After your father then. The Admiral in whose debt I shall forever be.

Penn: As you wish: Pennsylvania.

King: Now according to this document you must send to me two beaver skins to be delivered at our home, Windsor Castle, on the first day of January every year, and of course, one-fifth of all the gold and silver you may find.

Penn: Happily.

(They both sign the document, and Penn takes it under his arm.)

Penn: My colony will be a place where Quakers like me can live in peace, but people of all religions will be welcome.

(He unrolls the document and reads in a loud voice.)

Penn: Wanted: brave adventurers who wish to form a free colony for all people! Must be willing to travel 3,000 miles across the ocean. Must be willing to work hard and treat everyone as an equal! 5,000 acres for sale!

(One of the colonists, Margaret, stands up.)

Margaret: Count me in! I would like to live in a land where I can practice my religion freely, where I don't need to hide when I pray because I am a Quaker.

(Two other colonists, Samuel and Samantha, stand up.)

Samantha: We'll go! We've been wanting to start a family in a country where everyone is equal, no matter what their family background is.

Samuel: Where do we sign?

Penn: Right here.

(Two other colonists, Ben and Sarah, stand up.)

Ben: We'd like to go but we can't afford a high price.

Sarah: We don't have a lot of money.

Penn: Rent up to 200 acres at a penny an acre!

Ben and Sarah: Can we borrow that quill?

(They sign up.)

(Everyone gives coins to Penn as they move from this area to the ship area, lining up to board the boat.)

Penn: Be prepared for hardships!

Margaret and Samantha: *(together)* We have hardships here. We can't speak out without fear of being jailed for our beliefs.

Penn: Our boat, the Welcome is ready!

(He unrolls the Welcome *banner and hangs it aboard the ship. Everyone stands on board swaying slightly through this scene to show that they are at sea.)*

Ben: Cows and chickens are safely in their cages!

Sarah: The furniture is roped in tight!

Samuel: The *Welcome* is a strong ship.

Margaret: William Penn's three horses are safe!

Samantha: The *Welcome* is 108 feet long with three strong sails—a very seaworthy vessel.

Ben: A hundred colonists are safely aboard!

Penn: And I have the most precious cargo of all: THE CHARTER OF LIBERTY.

(Penn reads from a new parchment.)

Penn: What I have in my hand is a plan for good government. Our plans call for power to be placed in the hands of the people. To protect people from misuses of power, there are laws that must be followed for the good of all. I have written, "Liberty without obedience is confusion, and obedience without liberty is slavery."

(All repeat this line.)

Penn: "Let men be good, and the government cannot be bad..."

Samantha: There will be free elections in this new land. We will have a council and assembly that are chosen by the colonists.

Margaret: Our new set of forty laws includes freedom of worship, which is very important to so many of us Quakers who are aboard.

Ben: It also includes the right to a trial by jury.

Samuel: Nobody can be put to death in this new land except for murder or plotting to overthrow the government.

Margaret: With laws aboard we set sail happily.

Ben: (*talks to the audience*) Unfortunately, midway across the Atlantic Ocean, tragedy struck. A passenger came down with smallpox. In one week, 31 passengers died. Penn, who had already had the disease, went about the ship helping the sick.

Sarah: (*talks to the audience*) Seven weeks after we set sail we arrived in the new land, on October 24, 1682.

Margaret: We are in Pennsylvania!

Penn: Let us go up the river to the city I named Philadelphia, which means "Brotherly Love" in Greek.

Samuel: What shall we find in Philadelphia?

Penn: I have sent planners ahead of us and told them to begin building a city where houses have "ground on each side for gardens and orchards and fields."

Margaret: I have always wanted to live in a city which has parks and greenery.

Sarah: I would think that the greenery would help protect us from chimney fires and wind.

Penn: Yes, it is both beautiful to the eye and safer for the people who live there. Shall we leave the ship?

Ben: Lower the gang plank if you please!

(*All depart from the ship area. They are now in Philadelphia.*)

Penn: One of the first items of business for our new city will be to visit the Native Americans. Other colonists have not always treated them well. As a Quaker, I regard all people as equals and aim to live together with them in peace.

Samuel: May I go with you when you visit?

Penn: Yes, but you must leave all weapons at home.

Samuel: I carry only a hunting gun, William.

Penn: Still, there must be no weapons, whatsoever. It is a matter of respect.

Samuel: All right. I agree.

Samantha: Can you teach us how to speak to the Native Americans?

Penn: First you should know that our Pennsylvania is home to three peoples: the Lenni Lenape, the Susquehannock and the Shawnee. It will take time to learn their language but today I shall teach you one important word, *netap*.

All: *Netap.*

Ben: What does *netap* mean?

Penn: It is a word that will be important to all of us: "friend."

All: *Netap.*

Margaret: I have learned two new words on my first day in this new world of America. *Netap* or "friend," and *adelphos*, meaning "brother" in Greek.

Penn: I think we are off to a good start in Pennsylvania.

Samantha: Don't forget another important word, the word under which we sailed to this new land: WELCOME.

Penn: Yes, let us welcome all of those who wish to come to Pennsylvania and live in peace and harmony.

All: Welcome.

THE END

William Penn, and other Quaker colonists in Pennsylvania, believed in treating Native Americans with respect. Penn paid the Native Americans for their land, and relations with them remained peaceful for many years.

Poor Richard's Almanack

by Benjamin Franklin, 1732–1757

In the 13 English colonies, there were no television or radio news shows to tell people what the weather would be like each day or when community events such as fairs would take place. Instead, people depended on little booklets called almanacs for such information. Because almanacs were so popular among the colonists, many printers wrote their own versions and competed with one another for buyers. When Benjamin Franklin (1706–1790) first printed his Poor Richard's Almanack in 1732, there were at least six other almanacs on sale in Philadelphia alone. Yet Franklin's almanac quickly became the most popular in the English colonies because he included many clever and funny sayings. How do the sayings below help us to understand some of the ideas and values that English colonists considered important?

When the well's dry, we know the worth of water.

Keep conscience clear, Then never fear.

Three may keep a secret, if two of them are dead.

He that is of opinion money will do every thing may well be suspected of doing every thing for money.

Wish not so much to live long, as to live well.

If your head is wax, don't walk in the sun.

Plough deep while sluggards sleep; and you shall have corn to sell and to keep.

Genius without education
is like silver in the mine.

Well done, is twice done.

The family of fools is ancient.

Men and melons are hard to know.

Lost time is never found again.

An empty bag cannot stand upright.

Glass, china, and reputation, are easily
crack'd, and never well mended.

Little strokes, Fell great oaks.

Dost thou love life? Then do not squander
time; for that's the stuff life is made of.

There are three things extremely hard, steel,
a diamond and to know one's self.

Being ignorant is not so much a shame,
as being unwilling to learn.

Don't throw stones at your neighbors', if
your own windows are glass.

The honey is sweet, but the bee has a sting.

Where there is hunger, law is not regarded; and where
law is not regarded, there will be hunger.

A slip of the foot you may soon recover, but a slip
of the tongue you may never get over.

Paintings and fightings are best seen at a distance.

Ben Franklin continued to publish Poor Richard's Almanack *until 1757. From then until he died in 1790, Franklin was an important leader in the colonies and in the struggle for independence from England.*

Source: Benjamin Franklin, *Poor Richard's Almanack*. Mount Vernon, NY: The Peter Pauper Press, n.d.

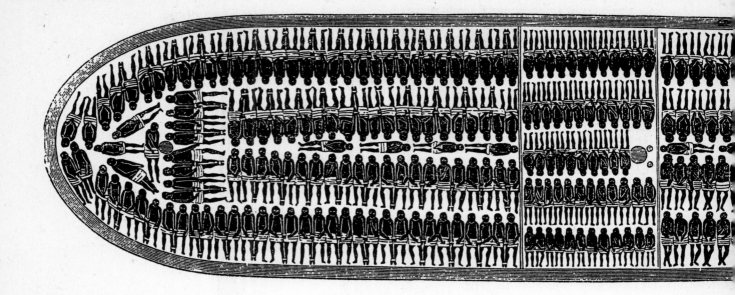

SHIP OF HORRORS

by Olaudah Equiano, 1789

By the late 1600s, slavery existed throughout the English colonies. For the slave traders, buying and selling human beings was a money-making business. But for the Africans kidnapped from their homeland, the forced ocean voyage to the Americas involved some of the greatest horrors that human beings have ever endured. In the excerpt below, adapted from his autobiography written in 1789, Olaudah Equiano (1745-1797) describes some of these horrors. Olaudah was an 11-year-old boy living in West Africa in 1756 when slave traders kidnapped him in order to take him to North America. The excerpt begins just as Olaudah arrives at the coast of Africa, about to begin the overseas voyage. What are some of the reactions of Olaudah and the other prisoners to the way in which they are treated? What are some of the things Olaudah wishes for?

The first thing I saw when I arrived at the coast was the sea and a slave ship waiting to pick up its cargo. The sight of the slave ship amazed me. This amazement turned into terror when I was carried on board. The crew immediately grabbed me and tossed me in the air to see if I was healthy. I was now convinced that I had gotten into a world of bad spirits and that they were going to kill me. The fact that their skin color differed so much from ours, that their hair was so long, and that the language they spoke was unlike any I had ever heard, strengthened my belief that they planned to kill me. I was so filled with horror and fear at that moment that if I had possessed 10,000 worlds, I would have given them all away to trade places with the poorest slave in my own country.

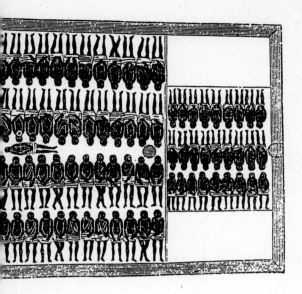

When I looked around the ship and saw large numbers of black people chained together—every one of them looking sad and unhappy—I no longer doubted my fate. Overpowered by horror and fright, I fell on the deck and fainted. When I woke up I was surrounded by black people. I asked them if these white men with their long hair and horrible looks were going to eat us up. They told me no. They tried to cheer me up, but I still felt miserable.

I now realized I would never again return to my native country. Never again would I see the shores of Africa. As I was realizing all of this, the crew sent me to the lower decks of the ship. Everybody down there was crying and the smell was worse than anything I had ever smelled in my life. It was so bad I became sick and could not eat. I did not feel like tasting a thing. I now wished only for death. At that moment two white men offered me food. When I refused they grabbed my hands, stretched me across a barrel, tied my feet, and whipped me.

Never in my life had I been treated in this way. As much as I feared drowning, I thought of jumping overboard. But the ship had nets all around it to prevent people from jumping into the ocean. Also, those prisoners who were not chained down were watched very closely by the crew to keep them from jumping overboard. Some prisoners who tried were beaten, and those who refused to eat were whipped every hour. This was often the case with myself.

A little later I came across some people from my own nation. Although we were all in chains, seeing them made me feel better. I asked them what was going to happen to us. They told me we were being carried to the white people's country to work for them. This cheered me up a little. After all, if all I had to do was work then things could not be so bad. But I still feared I would be put to death. The white people, I thought, looked and acted like savages. I had never seen such brutal cruelty in my life. They acted this way not only toward us blacks but toward each other. I saw them whip one white man so cruelly with a large rope that he died as a result. Then they tossed him over the side of the boat like an animal. This made me fear these people all the more, for I expected to be treated in the same manner.

After all the cargo was loaded, the smell in the lower decks became even worse. Everybody dripped with sweat and the air became unfit for breathing. We were packed together in chains so tightly we could hardly move or turn over. The cramped surroundings and the deadly heat almost suffocated us. Many slaves fell sick and died—a result of being packed so closely. The only reason they were packed so closely was to increase the profits of the slave dealers. This wretched situation was made even worse by the scraping of the chains. Children often fell into the tubs used for bathrooms and almost choked to death. The shrieks of the women and the groans of the dying made this scene a horror beyond belief.

One day the crew caught a large number of fish and feasted upon them. We begged and prayed for some of the fish that were left over. But to our amazement, they refused to give us any. Instead, they threw the fish overboard! Before they did this, however, some of my countrymen who were starving tried to grab some of the fish when they thought no one was looking. But they were discovered and whipped horribly.

One day, when the sea was smooth and the wind mild, two prisoners decided they would rather die than endure such a life of misery. Although they were chained together, they somehow managed to jump beyond the nets and into the sea. Immediately, another prisoner also jumped overboard. I believe many more would have done the some thing if the crew had not prevented them. The boat stopped at once to pick up the three prisoners who had jumped into the sea. The first two had drowned but they rescued the last one. They later whipped him extra cruelly for preferring death to slavery. In this manner we continued to undergo more hardships than I can now describe. These hardships were all caused by the wretched and terrible slave trade.

Olaudah Equiano was one of hundreds of thousands of Africans kidnapped and brought by force to North America at the hands of slave traders in the 1600s and 1700s. Roughly 200,000 more died on the ocean voyage. Equiano survived the voyage and worked as a slave in both Barbados, an island in the Caribbean, and the colony of Virginia. A British sea captain soon bought him and made him a sailor. Although enslaved, Equiano managed to earn money and bought his freedom in 1766. As a free man, he traveled the world and explored the northern Arctic. Years later he settled in England and wrote his autobiography. The book was widely read in the 1790s and contributed to the growth of the anti-slavery movement.

Source: Adapted from Olaudah Equiano, *The Interesting Narrative of the Life of Olaudah Equiano, or Gustavus Vassa, the African. Written by Himself.* New York: W. Durell, 1791.

SLAVE SALES

Advertisements, 1700s

During the 1700s European and American merchants forcibly transported more Africans to American shores than in any other century. Once these Africans arrived they were sold as slaves—and they could be resold at any time. As a result, slave sales were common events in the New England, Middle, and Southern colonies. Below is a selection of advertisements from newspapers and posters that appeared in colonial America. (Note that the letter s sometimes appeared as ſ.) How do these advertisements attempt to deprive Africans and African Americans of their humanity? How did one of these African Americans try to escape slavery?

TO BE SOLD on board the Ship *Bance-Ifland*, on tuefday the 6th of *May* next, at *Afhley-Ferry* ; a choice cargo of about 250 fine healthy

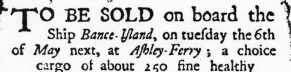

NEGROES,

juft arrived from the Windward & Rice Coaft. —The utmoft care has already been taken, and fhall be continued, to keep them free from the leaft danger of being infected with the SMALL-POX, no boat having been on board, and all other communication with people from *Charles-Town* prevented.

Auftin, Laurens, & Appleby.

N. B. Full one Half of the above Negroes have had the SMALL-POX in their own Country.

RUN away, on the 3d Day of *May* laft, a young Negro Boy, named *Joe*, this Country born, formerly belonged to Capt. *Hugh Heft*. Whoever brings the faid Boy the Subfcriber at *Edifto*, or to the Work Houfe in *Charles Town*, fhall have 3 *l* reward. On the contrary whoever harbours the faid Boy, may depend upon being feverely profecuted, by

Thomas Chifham.

TO BE SOLD,
A Likely negro Man, his Wife and Child ; the negro Man capable of doing all forts of Plantation Work, and a good Miller : The Woman exceeding fit for a Farmer, being capable of doing any Work, belonging to a Houfe in the Country, at reafonable Rates, inquire of the Printer hereof.

TO BE SOLD by William Yeomans, (in *Charles Town Merchant,*) a parcel of good Plantation Slaves. Encouragement will be given by taking Rice in Payment, or any Time Credit, Security to be given if required There's likewife to be fold, very good Troopleg faddles and Furniture, choice Barbados and Bofton Rum, alfo Cordial Waters and Limejuice, as well as a parcel of extraordinary Indian trading Goods, and many of other forts fuitable for the Seafon.

In the late 1700s slavery slowly began to die out in the North. Sales of enslaved people, however, continued to be daily events in the South until after the Civil War.

Father Junípero Serra

by Ivy Bolton, 1952

In 1769 a Spanish priest named Father Junípero Serra (hoo NEE pair roh SEH rah) came on foot from Mexico to build a series of missions throughout California. In this excerpt from a biography of Father Serra, the priest is on his way to found his first mission in California, San Diego. According to this biographer, what kind of man was Father Serra?

"This is sheer folly. You can go no farther, Father Serra. How could you ever have hoped to do missionary work in the wilds of Upper California with a leg like that? Look at it! I shall make a **litter** and send four men with you to carry you home." Comandante Portolá spoke with his usual decision.

> **litter:** kind of stretcher, or cot, to carry the sick

Father Serra stretched out the leg obediently and looked at it with a rueful smile. His face was white with fatigue and pain, but there was laughter still in his dark eyes and the little quirk at the side of his mouth told his **exasperated** commander that, as usual, Father Serra was finding something amusing in a situation which was not funny at all. He did not realize that his own excitement was the cause of the laughter now.

> **exasperated:** frustrated

The leg was a sorry sight, swollen and inflamed from knee to toe, with an open sore from the ankle halfway up the leg.

"It is one of the only two that I possess," Father Serra answered thoughtfully. "There is no need for all this worry, Comandante. The leg has been in this state, more or less, all the years I have been in the New World. I admit that at present it is a little more. God has called me to preach and found missions and I can trust Him to help me to do the task. He knows all about this handicap and has enabled me to come twelve hundred **leagues**. Surely, I can trust Him to get me the rest of the way."

> **leagues:** units of measure; one league equals about 3 miles

"And you will not go home? You should have had a doctor long ago."

"I have had doctors and none of them have been able to help me," Father Serra answered quietly. "This is the first present that the New World gave to me. Father Pedro and I were walking from **Vera Cruz** to Mexico City when the snake crossed our path. It struck at me and then went about its business in the undergrowth. The walk that afternoon was somewhat of an **ordeal** and the place has never healed. Wise doctors have told me that most people die of a similar snake bite. God had something for me to do and I lived. The 'something' is here in California and I have not the slightest **intention** of going home. If I delay you too much, leave me here with a little food and I will follow you with what speed I can."

> **Vera Cruz:** city on the Gulf coast of Mexico

> **ordeal:** difficult trial

> **intention:** idea of

"And run into Indians and wild beasts, not to mention more snakes," the comandante grumbled.

"I came here to find Indians and I am not afraid of snakes or wild beasts," Father Serra informed him. "Thus far we have seen nothing but desert, and the Indians, who are really important, must be looked for in good **earnest**. Leave off worrying. I shall be all right."

earnest: sincerity

Portolá pondered. "I am not going to leave you behind," he said obstinately and turned to summon two of his soldiers, who came running at his call.

"Cut wood and make a litter on which we can carry Father Serra," he commanded them. "Until you can walk again, that is what I intend to do and it is of no use for you to say any more, Father."

"Then I will not." Father Serra leaned back against a rock and surveyed the scene around him.

It was a glorious sight. In the west the sun was setting in a blaze of crimson and gold, the flaming cacti and desert plants greeted his beauty-loving eyes. The camp was being made ready and the men were gathering around the fires drawn by the scent of a cooking meal. Father Serra felt far too sick and weary to eat. He was grave enough now. Something had to be done, that was certain. He could not be a burden on the expedition. Men and animals had quite enough to do without adding the task of carrying a sick man.

One of the animals was in trouble. It was the mule that had gone lame yesterday. The beast was making no secret of its discomfort and was making life as hard as possible for the **muleteer** by kicks and squeals and struggles—together with futile efforts to bite his doctor. The muleteer was trying to **poultice** the open sore. Even at this distance, the smell of the ingredients of the steaming mass was overpowering.

muleteer: person who handles mules

poultice: apply medicine to

Father Serra watched, idly at first, then with real interest. He could sympathize with the mule. If the sore was anything like his own, no wonder the animal wanted to bite and kick.

The muleteer was skillful. His voice was going on in a murmur to reassure his patient. Very gradually the mule grew quieter. At last a bandage was fixed in place, and water and a nose bag were carried over to comfort the invalid.

The muleteer rose to his feet. "You will be able to go on tomorrow," he assured the mule and then turned to answer the call of Father Serra.

His dark eyes were full of concern as he saw the father's leg.

"My son, you know how to care for your animals," Father Serra said. "What can you do for my leg?"

"I know nothing about medicine, Father. I can cure a wound on a mule's back or a sore on its leg. You need a good doctor."

Father Serra laughed. "The doctors are twelve hundred leagues away and so I must have you. Make a remedy and apply it as you do to an animal. Pretend that I am a mule."

A snort behind him made Father Serra look around. His eyes met the sulky ones of Portolá.

"A good description?" Father Serra questioned, and the grim face of the comandante lightened a little.

"An excellent one," he agreed, and turned away.

The muleteer was still uneasy and unwilling to take the risk, but like everyone else in the expedition, he would do anything for Father Serra. All through the long trek over the scorching desert, when spirits were low, Father Serra could always inspire people with courage and his hand and strength were always at the service of a tired man.

"Go on, Juan," he urged the muleteer. "I need your help."

The muleteer went to work. He melted yellow **tallow** over the smoky fire and stirred in oil and herbs, a remedy no other man would have dared to try.

tallow: animal fat used to make candles

Even Father Serra clenched his hands and bit his lip to keep back a groan as the hot mass was laid on his open sore. His face grew whiter still and tears, forced out by sheer pain, made the eyes behind the glasses misty.

He managed a grateful "Thank you," when the leg was bandaged. He found himself lifted in strong arms and laid upon a couch of straw and leaves, which eager hands had made ready. The muleteer's cloak was rolled up for a pillow and a mule's blanket was used for a covering.

Juan brought broth and fed it to Father Serra by spoonfuls and then rose to his feet.

"The pain will be easier soon," he promised. "You will sleep. God grant that you are better in the morning."

"God grant it indeed," Father Serra murmured.

He lay quiet as the waves of pain engulfed him. Pain was no new experience to Father Serra. While he lay he prayed earnestly that God—who had brought him all this way to the land of his heart's desire—would make it possible for him to walk on. A missionary who had to be carried would delay the expedition badly. If the eyes of unseen Indians were watching—and almost certainly they were—would they ever listen to a man who was so helpless?

Oh, these were stupid thoughts, Father Serra decided. There were so many things that he had wanted to do which were out of his reach, things which had seemed utterly impossible at the time. Suddenly, in his own way, God had opened a path here, a friend there, and a great desire had been won.

By 1823 Father Serra had founded 21 missions in California, each only a day's journey apart, stretching all the way north to San Francisco.

Source: Ivy Bolton, *Father Junipero Serra*. New York: Julian Messner, Inc., 1952.

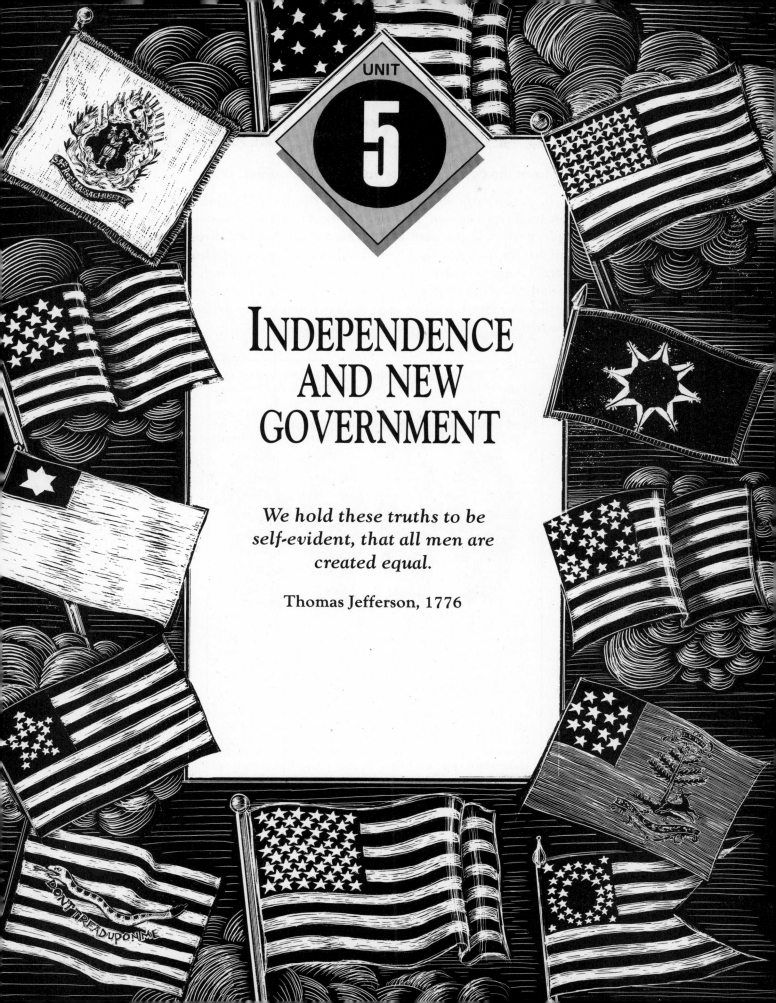

UNIT 5

INDEPENDENCE AND NEW GOVERNMENT

We hold these truths to be self-evident, that all men are created equal.

Thomas Jefferson, 1776

The Boston Massacre

from the Boston *Gazette and Country Journal*, 1770

On March 5, 1770, a crowd of colonists gathered in Boston and began hurling rocks at a group of British soldiers. Angered, the soldiers fired into the crowd—instantly killing four people. Outraged colonists called this a massacre, and three days later thousands turned out for the funeral. The following newspaper article appeared in the Boston Gazette and Country Journal. Look at the original version below and then read the modern translation on the next page. (Notice that in the original article, the letter ſ is often used in place of an s.) In what ways does the newspaper article try to shape the reader's opinions?

Laſt Thurſday, agreeable to a general Requeſt of the Inhabitants, and by the Conſent of Parents and Friends, were carried to their *Grave* in Succeſſion, the Bodies of *Samuel Gray, Samuel Maverick, James Caldwell,* and *Criſpus Attucks,* the unhappy Victims who fell in the bloody Maſſacre of the Monday Evening preceeding !

On this Occaſion moſt of the Shops in Town were ſhut, all the Bells were ordered to toll a ſolemn Peal, as were alſo thoſe in the neighboring Towns of Charleſtown Roxbury, &c. The Proceſſion began to move between the Hours of 4 and 5 in the Afternoon ; two of the unfortunate Sufferers, viz. Meſſ. *James Caldwell* and *Criſpus Attucks,* who were Strangers, borne from Faneuil-Hall, attended by a numerous Train of Perſons of all Ranks ; and the other two, viz. Mr. *Samuel Gray,* from the Houſe of Mr. Benjamin Gray, (his Brother) on the North-ſide the Exchange, and Mr. *Maverick,* from the Houſe of his diſtreſſed Mother Mrs. *Mary Maverick,* in Union-Street, each followed by their reſpective Relations and Friends : The ſeveral Hearſes forming a Junction in King-Street, the Theatre of that inhuman Tragedy ! proceeded from thence thro' the Main-Street, lengthened by an immenſe Concourſe of People, ſo numerous as to be obliged to follow in Ranks of ſix, and brought up by a long Train of Carriages belonging to the principal Gentry of the Town. The Bodies were depoſited in one Vault in the middle Burying-ground : The aggravated Circumſtances of their Death, the Diſtreſs and Sorrow viſible in every Countenance, together with the peculiar Solemnity with which the whole Funeral was conducted, ſurpaſs Deſcription.

Last Thursday, the bodies of Samuel Gray, Samuel Maverick, James Caldwell, and Crispus Attucks were carried to their graves. All four had died the unhappy victims of the bloody massacre three days earlier! Local citizens had requested a public funeral, and the victims' parents and friends agreed to it.

The funeral procession began between 4:00 and 5:00 in the afternoon. Most of the stores in town were closed, and all the bells in Boston, Charlestown, Roxbury, and elsewhere rang solemnly in honor of the dead. Two of the unfortunate sufferers, James Caldwell and Crispus Attucks, were both unknown in Boston. Beginning at Faneuil (fan′ yəl) Hall, a group made up of all kinds of people marched behind their coffins. A second group of people marched from the house of Samuel Gray's brother, and a third from the house of Samuel Maverick's very sad mother. The three groups came together at King Street, where the terrible tragedy had taken place! The procession then continued down Main Street. Huge crowds of people joined the march—so many, in fact, that they had to walk in rows of six people across. The procession was completed by a long train of carriages owned by the town's wealthier people. The bodies were at last buried in the ground. The alarming way in which the victims died, the sadness visible on everyone's faces, and the seriousness of the entire funeral are beyond description.

About 10,000 of Boston's 16,000 people turned out for the funeral. This heavy turnout was very surprising because two of those killed—a pair of sailors named James Caldwell and Crispus Attucks, a former slave—knew very few people in Boston. Newspapers all over the colonies reported the funeral, and the event that became known as the Boston Massacre increased colonists' anger against the British. As tensions between Britain and the American colonies grew during the next few years, many newspapers printed articles in favor of independence.

Source: Boston *Gazette and Country Journal*, March 12, 1770.

Paul Revere's Ride

by Henry Wadsworth Longfellow, 1863

Every country has its heroes and a body of literature that celebrates their heroic deeds. In 1861, the poet Henry Wadsworth Longfellow remembered Paul Revere and his midnight ride. Revere, a silversmith and soldier, was a leading member of the Sons of Liberty. Less than twenty-four hours before the shots that marked the beginning of the Revolutionary War, Revere and two other Patriots galloped across the countryside. They warned the sleeping citizens of Middlesex and Concord of the upcoming British attack. What do you think would have happened had the midnight riders failed to deliver their message to their countrymen?

Listen, my children, and you shall hear
Of the midnight ride of Paul Revere,
On the eighteenth of April, in Seventy-five;
Hardly a man is now alive
Who remembers that famous day and year.

He said to his friend, "If the British march
By land or sea from **the town** tonight,
Hang a lantern aloft in the **belfry** arch
Of the North Church tower as a signal light,—
One, if by land, and two, if by sea;
And I on the opposite shore will be,
Ready to ride and spread the alarm
Through every **Middlesex** village and farm,
For the country folk to be up and to arm."

Then he said, "Good-night!" and with **muffled** oar
Silently rowed to the Charlestown shore.
Just as the moon rose over the bay,
Where swinging wide at her **moorings** lay
The *Somerset*, British **man-of-war**;
A phantom ship, with each mast and **spar**
Across the moon like a prison bar,
And a huge black hulk, that was magnified
By its own reflection in the tide.

Meanwhile, his friend, through alley and street,
Wanders and watches with eager ears.
Till in the silence around him he hears
The **muster** of men at the **barrack** door,
The sound of arms, and the tramp of feet,
And the measured tread of the **grenadiers**,
Marching down to their boats on the shore.

He: Paul Revere
the town: Boston
belfry: bell tower

Middlesex: county north of Boston, including Lexington and Concord

muffled: quiet, perhaps wrapped in cloth to reduce the sound

moorings: ropes and anchors keeping a ship in place
man-of-war: warship
spar: pole that holds a ship's sails

muster: gathering
barrack: housing for soldiers
grenadiers: soldiers

Then he climbed the tower of the Old North Church,
By the wooden stairs, with stealthy tread,
To the belfry-chamber overhead,
And startled the pigeons from their perch
On the **sombre** rafters, that round him made
Masses and moving shapes of shade,—
By the trembling ladder, steep and tall,
To the highest window in the wall,
Where he paused to listen and look down
A moment on the roofs of the town,
And the moonlight flowing over all.

Beneath, in the churchyard, lay the dead,
In their **night-encampment** on the hill,
Wrapped in silence so deep and still
That he could hear, like a **sentinel's** tread,
The watchful night-wind, as it went
Creeping along from tent to tent.
And seeming to whisper, "All is well!"
A moment only he feels the spell
Of the place and the hour, and the secret dread
Of the lonely belfry and the dead;
For suddenly all his thoughts are bent
On a shadowy something far away,
Where the river widens to meet the bay,—
A line of black that bends and floats
On the rising tide, like a bridge of boats.

Meanwhile, impatient to mount and ride,
Booted and spurred, with a heavy stride
On the opposite shore walked Paul Revere.
Now he patted his horse's side,
Now gazed at the landscape far and near,
Then, impetuous, stamped the earth,
And turned and tightened his **saddle-girth**;
But mostly he watched with eager search
The belfry-tower of the Old North Church,
As it rose above the graves on the hill,
Lonely and **spectral** and sombre and still.
And **lo**! as he looks, on the belfry's height
A glimmer, and then a gleam of light!
He springs to the saddle, the bridle he turns,
But lingers and gazes, till full on his sight
A second lamp in the belfry burns!

sombre: (English spelling of *somber*) gloomy

night-encampment: cemetery

sentinel's: guard's or watchman's

Booted and spurred: wearing boots and spurs

saddle-girth: belt that holds a saddle on the horse

spectral: ghostly

lo: look

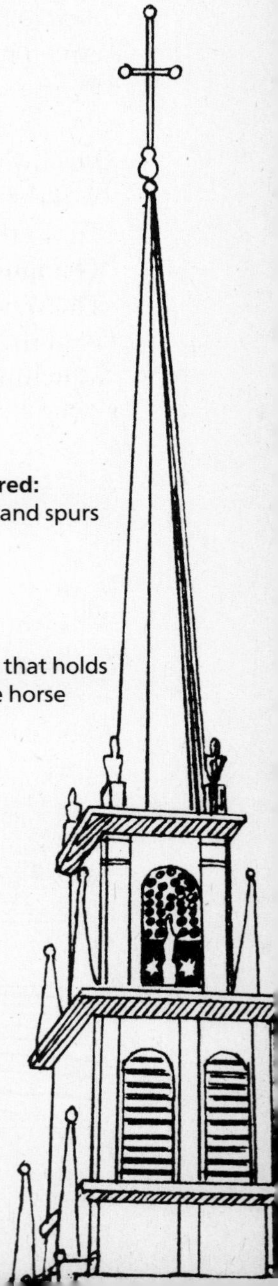

A hurry of hoofs in a village street,
A shape in the moonlight, a bulk in the dark,
And beneath, from the pebbles, in passing a spark
Struck out by a steed flying fearless and fleet:
That was all! And yet, through the gloom and the light,
The fate of a nation was riding that night;
And the spark struck out by that steed in his flight,
Kindled the land into flame with its heat.

He has left the village and **mounted the steep**,
And beneath him, tranquil and broad and deep,
Is the **Mystic**, meeting the ocean tides;
And under the **alders** that skirt its edge,
Now soft on the sand, now loud on the ledge,
Is heard the tramp of his steed as he rides.

mounted the steep: climbed the hill

Mystic: river running through Medford, Massachusetts

alders: type of trees

It was twelve by the village clock,
When he crossed the bridge into Medford town.
He heard the crowing of the cock,
And the barking of the farmer's dog,
And felt the damp of the river fog
That rises after the sun goes down.

It was one by the village clock,
When he galloped into Lexington.
He saw the **gilded weathercock**
Swim in the moonlight as he passed,
And the meeting-house windows, blank and bare,
Gaze at him with a spectral glare,
As if they already stood aghast
At the bloody work they would look upon.

gilded weathercock: gold-coated weather vane shaped like a rooster

It was two by the village clock,
When he came to the bridge in Concord town.
He heard the **bleating of the flock**,
And the twitter of birds among the trees,
And felt the breath of the morning breeze
Blowing over the meadows brown.
And one was safe and asleep in his bed
Who at the bridge would be first to fall,
Who that day would be lying dead,
Pierced by a British musket-ball.

bleating of the flock: crying of sheep

You know the rest. In the books you have read,
How the British Regulars fired and fled,—
How the farmers gave them ball for ball,
From behind each fence and farm-yard wall,
Chasing the red-coats down the lane,
Then crossing the fields to emerge again
Under the trees at the turn of the road,
And only pausing to fire and load.

So through the night rode Paul Revere;
And so through the night went his cry of alarm
To every Middlesex village and farm,—
A cry of defiance and not of fear,
A voice in the darkness, a knock at the door,
And a word that shall echo forevermore!
For, **borne** on the night-wind of the Past,   **borne:** carried
Through all our history, to the last,
In the hour of darkness and peril and need,
The people will waken and listen to hear
The hurrying hoof-beats of that steed,
And the midnight message of Paul Revere.

Longfellow (1807–1882) was a professor of modern languages at Bowdoin and Harvard colleges. His work includes a number of long poems about historic events. He wrote "Paul Revere's Ride" in 1861, during the Civil War between the North and the South. Why do you think he might have written this poem at that time?

Source: George Gesner, ed., *Anthology of American Poetry*. New York: Avenel Books, 1983.

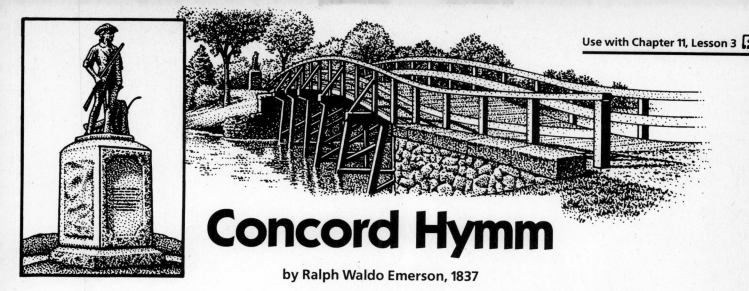

Concord Hymm

by Ralph Waldo Emerson, 1837

The battles of Lexington and Concord marked the beginning of the Revolutionary War. The writer and philosopher Ralph Waldo Emerson (1803–1882) wrote the poem "Concord Hymn" for the unveiling of a monument to the patriots of Concord. It was first sung as a hymn at the 1837 ceremony and was later distributed as a printed leaflet. In 1876 it was published in Emerson's book of Selected Poems. Emerson's poem has since been read by millions of schoolchildren. What did Emerson mean by the phrase "the shot heard round the world"?

July 4, 1837

By the **rude** bridge that arched the flood,
    Their flag to April's breeze unfurled,
Here once the embattled farmers stood
    And fired the shot heard round the world.

rude: simple, rustic

The foe long since in silence slept;
    Alike the conqueror silent sleeps;
And Time the ruined bridge has swept
    Down the dark stream which seaward creeps.

On this green bank, by this soft stream,
    We set to-day a **votive** stone;
That memory may their deed **redeem**,
    When, like our **sires**, our sons are gone.

votive: in fulfillment of a promise or vow
redeem: reclaim
sires: fathers, parents

Spirit, that made those heroes dare
    To die, and leave their children free,
Bid Time and Nature gently spare
    The shaft we raise to them and thee.

The poem is dated July 4, 1837, in honor of Independence Day. The colonies could not have achieved their independence from Britain without the blood that was shed at Lexington and Concord. Emerson's poem expresses the bittersweet feelings of pride in the Patriots and sorrow for the heroes who gave their lives for freedom.

Source: Sculley Bradley, Richmond Croom Beatty, E. Hudson Long, and George Perkins, eds., *The American Tradition in Literature*, Fifth Edition. New York: Random House, 1981.

Declaration of Independence

by Thomas Jefferson, 1776

By the spring of 1776, American colonists had been at war with Britian for about a year. During that time colonists debated whether they were fighting for more rights from Britain or for total independence. As the fighting went on, more and more colonists argued that peace with Britain was no longer possible. In June 1776 members of the Second Continental Congress asked 33-year-old Thomas Jefferson (1743–1826) of Virginia to write a statement explaining why the colonies ought to be independent. Read the Declaration of Independence that Jefferson wrote and the notes of explanation beside it. Notice Jefferson's ideas about government, rebellion, and people's rights. Notice also what injustices he accuses King George III of Great Britain of having committed against the colonists. How do King George's actions take away the rights that Jefferson believes people and governments should have?

When in the Course of human events,

it becomes necessary for one people to dissolve the political bands which have connected them with another, and to assume, among the Powers of the earth, the separate and equal station to which the Laws of Nature and of Nature's God entitle them, a decent respect to the opinions of mankind requires that they should declare the causes which impel them to the separation.

At certain times in history, it is necessary for a group of people to break away from the government that has ruled them and to form a new, independent nation. At such a time, their reasons for separation and independence should be clearly stated.

We hold these truths to be self-evident, that all men are created equal, that they are endowed by their Creator with certain unalienable Rights, that among these are Life, Liberty, and the pursuit of Happiness.

We believe that everyone agrees on certain basic ideas: All people are created equal and they have basic rights that can never be taken away. People have the right to live, the right to be free, and the right to seek happiness.

That, to secure these rights, Governments are instituted among Men, deriving their just Powers from the consent of the governed.

That, whenever any Form of Government becomes destructive of these ends, it is the Right of the People to alter or to abolish it, and to institute new Government, laying its foundation on such Principles, and organizing its powers in such form, as to them shall seem most likely to effect their Safety and Happiness.

Prudence, indeed, will dictate that Governments long established should not be changed for light and transient causes; and, accordingly all experience hath shown, that mankind are more disposed to suffer, while evils are sufferable, than to right themselves by abolishing the forms to which they are accustomed. But, when a long train of abuses and usurpations, pursuing invariably the same Object, evinces a design to reduce them under absolute Despotism, it is their right, it is their duty, to throw off such Government, and to provide new Guards for their future security.

Such has been the patient sufferance of these Colonies; and such is now the necessity which constrains them to alter their former Systems of Government. The history of the present King of Great Britain is a history of repeated injuries and usurpations, all having in direct object the establishment of an absolute Tyranny over these States.

To prove this, let Facts be submitted to a candid world.

He has refused his Assent to Laws the most wholesome and necessary for the public good.

He has forbidden his Governors to pass Laws of immediate and pressing importance, unless suspended in their operation till his Assent should be obtained; and when so suspended, he has utterly neglected to attend to them.

He has refused to pass other Laws for the accommodation of large districts of People, unless those People would relinquish the right of Representation in the Legislature, a right inestimable to them and formidable to tyrants only.

He has called together legislative bodies at places unusual, uncomfortable, and distant from the depository of their Public Records, for the sole purpose of fatiguing them into compliance with his measures.

To preserve these rights, people create governments. Every government must have the support of the people it governs.

If a government loses this support or tries to take away basic freedoms, people have the right to change their government or to get rid of it and form a new government that will protect their rights.

However, people should not change governments that have long been in power for minor or temporary problems. We have learned from history that people are usually more willing to put up with a bad government than to get rid of it. But when people see their government misusing its power and mistreating its people time after time, it is the right and duty of the people to get rid of their government and to form a new one.

The colonies have suffered patiently long enough, and it is now time to change our government. King George III of Great Britain has ruled badly for many years. His main goal has been to establish total control over the colonies.

These statements are proven by the following facts:

King George III has rejected much-needed laws passed by the colonists.

He has not permitted important laws to be passed by his governors in the 13 English colonies.

He has refused to redraw the borders of large voting districts unless the people living there agreed to give up their right to be represented in the legislature.

He has ordered lawmakers in the colonies to meet far from their homes and offices in places that are unusual and difficult to get to. His only reason for doing this has been to tire out the lawmakers so that they will accept his rule.

He has dissolved Representative Houses repeatedly, for opposing, with manly firmness, his invasions on the rights of the people.

He has refused for a long time, after such dissolutions, to cause others to be elected; whereby the Legislative Powers, incapable of Annihilation, have returned to the People at large for their exercise; the State remaining in the mean time exposed to all the dangers of invasion from without, and convulsions within.

He has endeavoured to prevent the Population of these States; for that purpose obstructing the Laws of Naturalization of Foreigners; refusing to pass others to encourage their migration hither, and raising the conditions of new Appropriations of Lands.

He has obstructed the Administration of Justice, by refusing his Assent to Laws for establishing Judiciary Powers.

He has made Judges dependent on his Will alone, for the tenure of their offices, and the amount and payment of their salaries.

He has erected a multitude of New Offices, and sent hither swarms of Officers to harass our People, and eat out their substance.

He has kept among us, in times of Peace, Standing Armies, without the Consent of our legislature.

He has affected to render the Military independent of and superior to the Civil Power.

He has combined with others to subject us to a jurisdiction foreign to our constitution, and unacknowledged by our laws; giving his Assent to their Acts of pretended Legislation:

For quartering large bodies of armed troops among us:

For protecting them, by a mock Trial, from Punishment for any Murders which they should commit on the Inhabitants of these States:

For cutting off our Trade with all parts of the world:

When lawmakers have criticized the king for attacking their rights, he has broken up the legislature's meetings.

After breaking up their meetings, the king has refused to allow new elections. As a result, colonists have been living in danger, unable to protect themselves or pass new laws.

He has tried to stop colonists from moving west and settling in new lands. He has also tried to prevent people from foreign countries from settling in America by making it hard for newcomers to become citizens.

In some places, he has not let colonists set up a system of courts.

He has forced colonial judges to obey him by deciding how long they can serve and how much they are paid.

He has sent officials from Britain to fill new government offices in the colonies. These officials have mistreated people and demanded unfair taxes.

In times of peace he has kept soldiers in the colonies even though the colonists did not want them.

He has tried to give soldiers power over colonial legislatures.

He and other leaders in Great Britain have passed laws for the colonies that the colonists did not want. In these laws the British government has:

forced colonists to house and feed British soldiers;

protected these soldiers by giving them phony trials and not punishing them for murdering colonists;

cut off trade between colonists and people in other parts of the world;

For imposing Taxes on us without our Consent:

demanded taxes that colonists never agreed to;

For depriving us, in many cases, of the benefits of Trial by Jury:

prevented colonists accused of crimes from having their trials decided fairly by a jury;

For transporting us beyond Seas to be tried for pretended offences:

brought colonists falsely accused of crimes to Great Britain to be put on trial;

For abolishing the free System of English Laws in a neighbouring Province, establishing therein an Arbitrary government, and enlarging its Boundaries, so as to render it at once an example and fit instrument for introducing the same absolute rule into these Colonies:

extended the borders of the neighboring province of Quebec to include lands stretching to the Ohio River, thus forcing colonists in this region to obey harsh French laws rather than English laws. The goal of the British government is to force all colonists to obey these harsh laws;

For taking away our Charters, abolishing our most valuable Laws, and altering fundamentally the Forms of our Governments:

taken away our charters, or documents that make governments legal, canceled important laws, and completely changed our forms of government;

For suspending our own Legislatures, and declaring themselves invested with Power to legislate for us in all cases whatsoever.

broken up our legislatures and claimed that Great Britain has the right to pass all laws for the colonies.

He has abdicated Government here, by declaring us out of his Protection and waging War against us.

King George III has ended government in the colonies by waging war against us and not protecting us.

He has plundered our seas, ravaged our Coasts, burnt our towns, and destroyed the Lives of our People.

He has robbed colonists' ships at sea, burned down our towns, and ruined people's lives.

He is at this time transporting large Armies of foreign Mercenaries to compleat the works of death, desolation and tyranny, already begun with circumstances of Cruelty & perfidy scarcely paralleled in the most barbarous ages, and totally unworthy the Head of a civilized nation.

He is right now bringing foreign soldiers to the colonies to commit horrible and brutal deeds. These actions by the king are some of the cruelest ever committed in the history of the world.

He has constrained our fellow Citizens taken Captive on the high Seas to bear Arms against their Country, to become the executioners of their friends and Brethren, or to fall themselves by their Hands.

He has forced colonists captured at sea to join the British Navy and to fight and kill other colonists.

He has excited domestic insurrections amongst us, and has endeavoured to bring on the inhabitants of our frontiers, the merciless Indian Savages, whose known rule of warfare, is an undistinguished destruction of all ages, sexes and conditions.

He has urged enslaved people in the colonies to rebel, and he has tried to get Native Americans to fight against colonists.

In every stage of these Oppressions We have Petitioned for Redress in the most humble terms: Our repeated Petitions have been answered only by repeated injury. A Prince, whose character is thus marked by every act which may define a Tyrant, is unfit to be the ruler of a free People.

Nor have We been wanting in attention to our British brethren. We have warned them from time to time of attempts by their legislature to extend an unwarrantable jurisdiction over us. We have reminded them of the circumstances of our emigration and settlement here. We have appealed to their native justice and magnanimity, and we have conjured them by the ties of our common kindred to disavow these usurpations, which, would inevitably interrupt our connections and correspondence. They too have been deaf to the voice of justice and of consanguinity. We must, therefore, acquiesce in the necessity, which denounces our Separation, and hold them, as we hold the rest of mankind, Enemies in War, in Peace Friends.

We, therefore, the Representatives of the United States of America, in General Congress Assembled, appealing to the Supreme Judge of the world for the rectitude of our intentions, do, in the Name, and by Authority of the good People of these Colonies, solemnly publish and declare, That these United Colonies are, and of Right ought to be Free and Independent States; that they are Absolved from all Allegiance to the British Crown, and that all political connection between them and the State of Great Britain, is and ought to be totally dissolved; and that as Free and Independent States, they have full Power to levy War, conclude Peace, contract Alliances, establish Commerce, and to do all other Acts and Things which Independent States may of right do. And for the support of this Declaration, with a firm reliance on the protection of divine Providence, we mutually pledge to each other our Lives, our Fortunes and our sacred Honour.

For years we have asked King George III to correct these problems and safeguard our rights. Unfortunately, the king has refused to listen to our complaints and he continues to treat us badly. The king is such an unfair ruler that he is not fit to rule the free people of the 13 colonies.

We have also asked the British people for help. We have told them many times of our problems and pointed out the unfair laws passed by their government. We hoped they would listen to us because they believed in reason and justice. We hoped they would listen to us because we are related to each other and have much in common. But we were wrong: The British people have not listened to us at all. They have ignored our pleas for justice. We must, therefore, break away from Great Britain and become a separate nation.

In the name of the American people, we members of the Continental Congress declare that the United States of America is no longer a colony of Great Britain but is, instead, a free and independent nation. The United States now cuts off all its relations with Great Britain. As a free nation the United States has the right and power to make war and peace, make agreements with other nations, conduct trade, and do all the things that independent nations have the right to do. To support this Declaration of Independence, we promise to each other our lives, our fortunes, and our personal honor.

On July 4, 1776, the members of the Second Continental Congress approved the Declaration of Independence. This action made it clear that Americans were no longer colonists, but rather citizens of a new country called the United States of America. For more than 200 years, Jefferson's words have inspired people all over the world in their struggle for liberty and independence. To learn how African Americans applied some of the ideas in the Declaration of Independence, read their petition for freedom on pages 71–72.

Common Sense

by Thomas Paine, 1776

Thomas Paine was an American patriot (1737-1809) whose ability to express his ideas through the use of bold and graphic language made his political theories easily understandable to the public. In January 1776 Paine published a pamphlet called Common Sense. In this pamphlet, Paine argued for independence from Great Britain. He said that Great Britain's rule was not kindly. Further, he wrote that the colonies had nothing to lose by leaving the British empire since Britain was too far away to rule effectively. In just three months the colonists bought nearly 12,000 copies of Common Sense. Why were the colonists ready to listen to Thomas Paine?

In the following pages I offer nothing more than simple facts, plain arguments, and common sense....

The sun never shined on a **cause** of greater worth.'Tis not the affair of a city, a county, a province, or a kingdom, but of a continent—of at least one eighth part of the **habitable** globe.'Tis not the concern of a day, a year, or an age; **posterity** are virtually involved in the contest, and will be more or less affected, even to the end of time, by the **proceedings** now. Now is the **seed-time** of continental union, faith and honor....

I have heard it asserted by some, that as America hath flourished under her former **connexion** with Great-Britain, that the same connexion is necessary towards her future happiness, and will always have the same effect. Nothing can be more **fallacious** than this kind of argument. We may as well assert that because a child has thrived upon milk, that it is never to have meat, or that the first twenty years of our lives is to become a **precedent** for the next twenty. But even this is admitting more than is true, for I answer **roundly**, that America would have flourished as much, and probably much more, had no European power had anything to do with her. The commerce, by which she hath enriched herself, are the **necessaries** of life, and will always have a market while eating is the custom of Europe.

But she has protected us, say some. That she has **engrossed** us is true, and defended the continent at our **expence** as well as her own is admitted, and she would have defended Turkey from the same motive, **viz.** the sake of trade and dominion....

cause: here refers to independence from Britain

habitable: livable

posterity: future generations

proceedings: events

seed-time: time when seed is planted for later harvest; that is, the beginning

connexion: connection, tie to

fallacious: false

precedent: model

roundly: confidently

necessaries: vital things

engrossed: enlarged

expence: expense

viz: that is

Europe is too thickly planted with kingdoms to be long at peace, and whenever a war breaks out between England and any foreign power, the trade of America goes to ruin, *because of her connection with Britain*.... Every thing that is right or natural pleads for separation. The blood of the slain, the weeping voice of nature cries, 'TIS TIME TO PART. Even the distance at which the **Almighty** hath placed England and America, is a strong and natural proof, that the authority of the one, over the other, was never the design of Heaven....

'TIS: it is
Almighty: God

As to government matters, it is not in the power of Britain to do this continent justice: The business of it will soon be too weighty, and intricate, to be managed with any tolerable degree of convenience, by a power so distant from us, and so very ignorant of us; for if they cannot conquer us, they cannot govern us. To be always running three or four thousand miles with a tale or a petition, waiting four or five months for an answer, which when obtained requires five or six more to explain it in, will in a few years be looked upon as **folly** and childishness—There was a time when it was proper, and there is a proper time for it to cease.

folly: foolishness

Small islands not capable of protecting themselves, are the proper objects for kingdoms to take under their care; but there is something very absurd, in supposing a continent to be perpetually governed by an island. In no instance hath nature made the **satellite larger than its primary planet**, and as England and America, with respect to each other, reverses the common order of nature, it is evident they belong to **different systems**; England to Europe, America to itself....

satellite ... planet: object in outer space that moves in a circle around larger objects; for example, the moon around Earth
different systems: any group of planets revolving around a star

TO CONCLUDE, however strange it may appear to some, or however unwilling they may be to think so, matters not, but many strong and striking reasons may be given, to **shew**, that nothing can settle our affairs so expeditiously as an open and determined declaration for independance....

shew: show

These proceedings may at first appear strange and difficult; but, like all other steps which we have already passed over, will in a little time become familiar and **agreeable**; and, until an independance is declared, the **Continent** will feel itself like a man who continues putting off some unpleasant business from day to day, yet knows it must be done, hates to set about it, wishes it over, and is continually haunted with the thoughts of its necessity.

agreeable: nice
Continent: America

In Common Sense, *Thomas Paine presented his arguments clearly and appealed to reason and common sense. Many say that his writings inspired two of the greatest revolutions in history—the American Revolution in 1776 and the French Revolution in 1789.*

Source: Thomas Paine, *Common Sense, The Rights of Man, and other Essential Writings of Thomas Paine*. New York: Meridian, 1984.

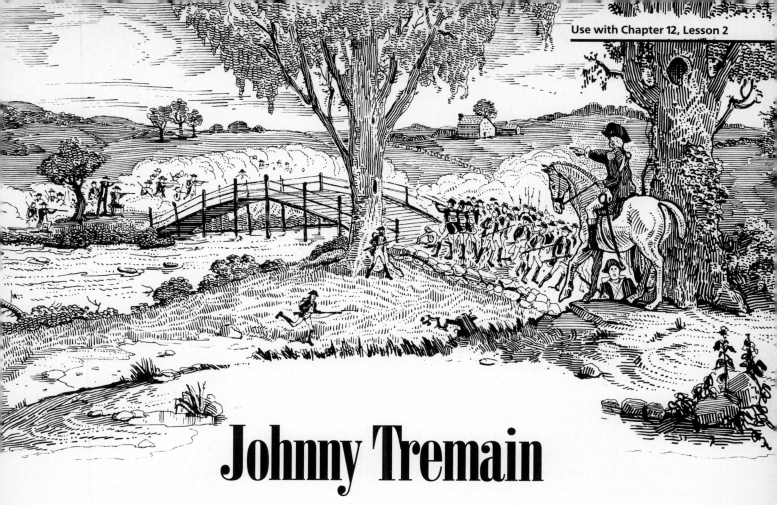

Johnny Tremain

by Esther Forbes, 1943

The English had a long history of fighting for liberty in their own country. In 1215 the Magna Carta, an early English charter of rights, limited the powers of the monarchy. In 1649 King Charles I was beheaded for abusing his power. In 1689 Parliament passed a Bill of Rights that increased the power of citizens. Thus, it was probably natural that the 13 English colonies in North America would eventually fight for the same kind of liberty. In the novel Johnny Tremain, the author depicts some of the major events that led up to the American Revolution as seen by a teenager growing up in Boston. This excerpt from the novel takes place in April 1775, immediately before the battles of Lexington and Concord. How does Johnny feel about the British?

Suddenly there was silence along the whole great length of the **brigade**. Slim Earl Percy on a white horse, escorted by a group of officers, was cantering slowly across the **Common**.

Five mounted men. The sun was bright that day with only breeze enough to **ruffle** the horses' manes, **flaunt** scarlet riding capes, float the flag of England. Johnny was an Englishman. The sullen, rebellious people standing about watching Percy and his staff approaching, waiting for the brigade to march, all were Englishmen. The flag—it stood for Magna Carta, the Bill of Rights, Charles the First's head upon a block, centuries of struggle for 'English liberty.' But over here there had grown up a broader interpretation of the

brigade: military unit
Common: village green

ruffle: disturb the calmness
flaunt: show off

word 'liberty': no man to be ruled or taxed except by men of his own choice. But we are still fighting for 'English liberty', and don't you forget it. French slaves to the north of us, Spanish slaves to the south of us. Only English colonies are allowed to taste the forbidden fruit of liberty—we who grew up under England. Johnny thought of **James Otis**'s words. Upholding the torch of liberty—which had been lighted on the fires of England.

James Otis: American patriot who opposed the Stamp Act

Not since the soldiers had come to Boston had Johnny removed his hat when the British flag went by except once when it had been knocked off his head by a soldier. He started to remove it now—for the first time and doubtless the last. Thought better of it—It was too late. He knew the shooting had begun.

The sword in Earl Percy's hand flashed. There was a command which was instantly picked up and repeated and echoed and repeated again. The **regimental** drummers struck up. The artillery horses threw their weight against their collars. Wagoners cracked their whips and the **scarlet dragon** swung forward, sluggishly at first, heading for the town gates. Thousands of separate feet merged into only one gigantic pair. Left, right, left, right. The earth shook to their rhythm. Johnny watched them pass. Every button was sewed on. Every buckle in place. Every cartridge box held exactly thirty-six cartridges. Every musket had a bayonet, and there was not one old **fowling piece** among them. Every horse had four new shoes. It was a magnificent sight, but Johnny felt a little sick.

regimental: belonging to a regiment, a military unit similar in size to a brigade

scarlet dragon: British brigade

fowling piece: gun for shooting fowl or birds

What chance—what shadow of a chance—had those poor, untrained, half-armed farmers at Concord? O God, be with us now. But even as he prayed, he kept an eye out for the regimental markings on the men's uniforms. It was the Fourth, the Twenty-Third, and the Forty-Seventh who were being sent out, plus five hundred marines, plus a small artillery train, and a few baggage wagons. Twelve hundred for a guess.

The drums throbbed. The heavy dragon marched on its thousands of feet, and now above the drums came the **shrilling** of **fifes**. They played a tune they always played when they wished to insult Yankees. For once more Yankee Doodle was going to town on a **spanking** stallion, with that forlorn feather in his cap, asking those **unmilitary questions**.

Poor Yankee Doodle. Whatever could he do against this great scarlet dragon?

shrilling: unpleasantly high-pitched sound

fifes: flutes

spanking: very nice, fancy

unmilitary questions: questions regarding independence from Britain

In this excerpt the author paints a vivid picture of the military might of the British redcoats that the colonists faced. Yet the colonists' desire for liberty was so strong that they eventually defeated the British and won their independence.

Source: Esther Forbes, *Johnny Tremain*. Santa Barbara, CA: Cornerstone Books, 1943.

A Petition for Freedom

by African Americans of Massachusetts, 1777

When the American Revolution began, slavery was legal in all 13 colonies. However, the aims and ideals of the Revolution—independence and freedom—were important to all Americans. During the 1770s African Americans in Massachusetts wrote many petitions to colonial leaders, seeking an end to slavery. The following 1777 petition to the new Massachusetts state government was signed by Prince Hall, a leading Boston minister, and seven other African Americans. As you read this excerpt, notice how the writers compare their struggle for freedom to the American struggle for independence from Great Britain. Which words and ideas in the petition can also be found in the Declaration of Independence, which you read on pages 62–66?

To the Honorable Counsel and House of Representatives for the State of Massachusetts Bay in General Court assembled, January 13, 1777

The petition of a great number of Blacks detained in a state of slavery in the **bowels** of a free and Christian country humbly show that your petitioners **apprehend** that they have in common with all other men a natural and **unalienable** right to that freedom which the Great Parent of the Universe hath **bestowed** equally on all mankind and which they have never **forfeited** by any compact or agreement whatever. But they were unjustly dragged by the hand of cruel power from their dearest friends and some of them even torn from the embraces of their tender parents—from a **populous**, pleasant, and plentiful country and in violation of laws of nature and of nations and in **defiance of** all the tender feelings of humanity brought here [to America] . . . to be sold like beasts of burden and like them condemned to slavery for life. . . . A life of slavery like that of your petitioners deprived of every social privilege of everything **requisite** to **render** life tolerable is far worse than **nonexistence**. . . .

Your petitioners have long and patiently waited the event of petition after petition by them presented to the legislative body

bowels: deepest parts
apprehend: understand

unalienable: incapable of being taken away
bestowed: given
forfeited: given up

populous: filled with people
defiance of: opposition to

requisite: necessary
render: make
nonexistence: death

of this state and [they] . . . **cannot but** express their astonishment   **cannot but:** can only
that it has never been considered that every principle from
which America has acted in the course of their unhappy
difficulties with Great Britain pleads stronger than a thousand
arguments in favor of your petitioners. They therefore humbly
beseech your honors to give this petition its due weight and   **beseech:** beg
consideration and cause an act of the Legislature to be passed
whereby they may be restored to the enjoyments of that which is
the natural right of all men—and [that] their children who were
born in this land of liberty may not to be held as slaves. . . .
And your petitioners, as in duty bound shall ever pray.

Lancaster Hill	Jack Purpont
Peter Bess	Nero Suneto
Brister Slenten	Newport Symner
Prince Hall	Job Lock

Lawmakers in Massachusetts ignored this petition for freedom just as they had ignored earlier petitions. Continued pressure by African Americans during the Revolutionary War, however, along with the ideals of the Revolution itself, led people in Massachusetts to end slavery in the 1780s. By 1800 most states in the North had outlawed slavery.

Source: *Collections of the Massachusetts Historical Society,* Vol. III, Fifth Series. Boston, 1877.

Song of Marion's Men

by William Cullen Bryant, 1831

The Revolutionary War was fought by resourceful men and women who drew upon their familiarity with the terrain to drive off the larger and professionally trained British army. One of these legendary Patriots was Captain Frances Marion (1732–1795), a brave South Carolinian who earned the nickname of "Swamp Fox." Marion's strategy was to make sneak, lightning-quick attacks on the British and then take cover in the swamps of Carolina. In 1831 the poet William Cullen Bryant wrote a poem in admiration of Marion's men. Marion's outfit was small, yet he and his men were highly successful. How do you think Marion's style of fighting differed from that of the British?

Our band is few but true and tried,
    Our leader frank and bold;
The British soldier trembles
    When Marion's name is told.
Our fortress is the good **greenwood**,   **greenwood:** forest
    Our tent the cypress-tree;
We know the forest round us,
    As seamen know the sea.
We know its walls of thorny vines,
    Its glades of reedy grass,
Its safe and silent islands
    Within the dark **morass**.   **morass:** swamp

Woe to the English soldiery
    That little dread us near!
On them shall light at midnight
    A strange and sudden fear:
When, waking to their tents on fire,
    They grasp their arms in vain,
And they who stand to face us
    Are beat to earth again;
And they who fly in terror deem
    A mighty host behind,
And hear the tramp of thousands

Upon the hollow wind.
Then sweet the hour that brings release
    From danger and from toil:
We talk the battle over,
    And share the battle's spoil.
The woodland rings with laugh and shout,
    As if a hunt were up,
And woodland flowers are gathered
    To crown the soldier's cup.
With merry songs we mock the wind
    That in the pine-top grieves,
And slumber long and sweetly
    On beds of oaken leaves.

Well knows the fair and friendly moon
    The band that Marion leads—
The glitter of their rifles,
    The scampering of their steeds.
'Tis life to guide the fiery **barb**
    Across the moonlight plain;
'Tis life to feel the night-wind
    That lifts the tossing mane.
A moment in the British camp—
    A moment—and away
Back to the pathless forest,
    Before the peep of day.

barb: horse

Grave men there are by broad **Santee,**
    Grave men with **hoary** hairs;
Their hearts are all with Marion,
    For Marion are their prayers.
And lovely ladies greet our band
    With kindliest welcoming,
With smiles like those of summer,
    And tears like those of spring.
For them we wear these trusty arms,
    And lay them down no more
Till we have driven the Briton,
    Forever, from our shore.

Santee: a river in South Carolina
hoary: ancient, old

William Cullen Bryant (1794–1878) was born in Cummington, Massachusetts. The poet and editor was part-owner of the newspaper The Evening Post. *Through his paper, Bryant voiced his support for an end to slavery and other reforms. He also translated the* Iliad *and the* Odyssey, *two great epic poems of the ancient Greeks. An epic poem is a narrative that tells of the deeds of a hero or of a nation. Although "Song of Marion's Men" is not as lengthy or ambitious as an epic, it has some of the same qualities. What deeds or characteristics of Marion and his band does the poem celebrate?*

Source: George Gesner, ed., *Anthology of American Poetry*. New York: Avenel Books, 1983.

Washington's Farewell to His Officers

from an eyewitness account by Benjamin Tallmadge, 1783

George Washington, Commander-in-Chief of the Continental Army, took an army of raw recruits and shaped them into a disciplined team. He fought with Congress for better pay to induce men to extend their term of service. Ultimately, he created an army that was able to defeat the British. By the time Washington bid farewell to his officers on December 4, 1783, he had become a military leader who was much loved by his troops. Why do you think this was so? The following excerpt is from an eyewitness account of this event, written by one of Washington's aides.

*T*he time now drew near when the Commander-in-Chief intended to leave this part of the country for his beloved retreat at Mount Vernon.

On Thursday, the 4th of December, it was made known to the officers then in New York that General Washington intended to commence his journey on that day. At 12 o'clock the Officers **repaired** to Fraunces Tavern, in Pearl Street, where General Washington had **appointed** to meet them, and to take his final

repaired: went

appointed: decided, named as the place

leave of them. We had assembled but a few moments, when his excellency entered the room. His emotion, too strong to be concealed, seemed to be **reciprocated** by every Officer present.

After **partaking** of a slight refreshment, in almost breathless silence, the General filled his glass with wine, and, turning to the Officers, he said: "With a heart full of love and gratitude, I now take leave of you. I most devoutly wish that your latter days may be as prosperous and happy as your former ones have been glorious and honorable."

After the Officers had taken a glass of wine, General Washington said: "I cannot come to each of you, but shall feel obliged if each of you will come and take me by the hand."

General Knox, being nearest to him, turned to the Commander-in-Chief, who, **suffused** in tears, was incapable of **utterance** but grasped his hand when they embraced each other in silence.

In the same affectionate manner, every Officer in the room marched up to, kissed, and parted with his General-in-Chief.

Such a scene of sorrow and weeping I had never before witnessed, and I hope may never be called upon to witness again. It was indeed too **affecting** to be of long **continuance**—for tears of deep **sensibility** filled every eye—and the heart seemed so full that it was ready to burst from its **wonted abode**. Not a word was uttered to break the solemn silence that **prevailed**, or to interrupt the tenderness of the interesting scene. The simple thought that we were then about to part from the man who had conducted us through a long and bloody war, and under whose conduct the glory and independence of our country had been achieved, and that we should see his face no more in this world, seemed to me utterly **insupportable**.

But the time of separation had come, and waving his hand to his grieving **children** around him, he left the room and, passing through a **corps** of **light infantry** who were paraded to receive him, he walked silently on the **whitehall**, where a barge was in waiting.

We all followed in mournful silence to the wharf, where a **prodigious** crowd had assembled to witness the departure of the man, who, under God, had been the great agent in establishing the glory and independence of these United States.

As soon as he was seated, the barge put off into the river, and, when out in the stream, our great and beloved General waved with hat, and **bid** us a silent **adieu**.

After the war Washington returned to Mount Vernon where he believed he would lead a peaceful life on his farm. This was not to be. The newly created United States was to call upon him again to lead their efforts to form a national government and to serve as our first President.

Source: Col. Benjamin Tallmadge, *Memoir of Colonel Benjamin Tallmadge*. New York: The New York Times & Arno Press, 1963.

reciprocated: returned equally

partaking: taking part

suffused: overflowing

utterance: talking

affecting: touching the emotions

continuance: duration

sensibility: feeling

wonted abode: usual home

prevailed: lasted

insupportable: unbearable

children: the officers, who look on Washington as a "father"

corps: military unit

light infantry: foot soldiers carrying small weapons

whitehall: boat dock

prodigious: large, huge

bid: offered

adieu: French for good-bye

Shh! We're Writing the Constitution

by Jean Fritz, 1987

In May 1787, 55 delegates from the 13 states met in Philadelphia at a Constitutional Convention. There they discussed problems that the states were having under the existing plan of government, the Articles of Confederation. In her book Shh! We're Writing the Constitution Jean Fritz makes this historical period come alive by painting vivid pictures with words of the drama and the personalities involved in writing the Constitution. In this excerpt from the book, the delegates debate fiercely over what kind of government the young country needs. They argue over whether to revise the Articles or to come up with a new plan entirely. Why do you think the debate was so fierce?

*I*f the people of the country were afraid of what might happen in the convention, so were the delegates themselves. They didn't call the document they were working on a "constitution"; they referred to it as "the plan." Because they knew that the country was sensitive to the word "national," they tried to stick to "federal," a word they were used to and one which didn't reduce the power of the states. But after Edmund Randolph, Governor of Virginia, had presented what came to be called the Virginia Plan, he spoke right out.

In the Virginia Plan, Randolph explained, there would be three branches of government. The executive branch would have a head who would be responsible for running the government. The legislative branch would be made up of two houses which would make laws. The House of Representatives would be elected directly by the people; the Senate, the smaller and supposedly more coolheaded body, would be elected by the House. Together they would be called the Congress. The third branch would be the judiciary headed by a Supreme Court, which would make sure that laws were constitutional and were properly obeyed.

Edmund Randolph was a tall, handsome, likable man and nothing he said at first seemed alarming. Some of the states had constitutions that were similar to the one he described. Besides, the members knew that after Randolph's plan had been discussed, other members would have a chance to present their plans. But at the end of his speech Randolph did **arouse** his audience. It should be clear, he said, that his resolutions were not merely for a federal government but for a national government that would be supreme over the states.

arouse: to cause an action or strong feeling

There was dead silence.

Pierce Butler of South Carolina was one of the first to recover. He jumped down hard on the word "national" but John Dickinson of Delaware said there was nothing wrong with the word. "We *are* a nation!" he declared.

No! For Elbridge Gerry of Massachusetts this kind of talk was scary. He was a thin, worrying sort of man who was sometimes called "Grumbletonian" behind his back. National? he sputtered. How could they think national? They had been sent here to revise the Articles of Confederation, not to destroy them.

As the meetings went on, all kinds of fear surfaced. The smaller states with fewer people were afraid of the larger states which had more people. In the past the votes of all states, no mater what their population, had counted the same. But a national government would be more concerned with individual people than with the states themselves. So what would happen to the small states now? And what kind of government were they forming? Some people were afraid of a **"high-toned"** or **aristocratic** government run by a small, privileged, wealthy group, the way a monarchy was usually run. Others were just as afraid of the common people having too much power. They weren't capable of governing, it was said.

high-toned: having to do with wealth and social position

aristocratic: born to a high social position

Eventually the convention did agree on a national legislature to consist of two houses but before final acceptance, the word "national" was crossed out.

Still, there were so many questions to decide. What about the person who was to be the executive or head of the government?

Should there be just one person? If so, would he seem like a king? Why not three people, each representing a different part of the country? But what if they fought among themselves? What if they couldn't reach an agreement? Should the executive be paid a salary? (Yes, said Madison. Don't count on patriotism.) But who should pay the salary—the states or the government of the United States? How should the executive be chosen? By the people? By the states? By a branch of the United States legislature? By **electors**? By **lot**? (They had to vote sixty times before they could settle this question.) And how long should the executive serve? If he were thought to be guilty of misconduct, could they **impeach** him? Could they remove him from office?

Alexander Hamilton was one of the few who wanted the president to serve a long term, perhaps even for life. He thought it would be embarrassing to watch a lot of ex-presidents wandering around like ghosts. But suppose you had a long-term president, Franklin pointed out. And suppose he turned out to be a bad president? What then? Out of simple kindness they ought to provide some way to get rid of him. Otherwise, Franklin chuckled, the only thing they could do would be to shoot him.

In the end it was decided that there should be a single executive who would be paid out of the Treasury of the new government. He

electors: people selected by a political party to vote in an election

lot: a piece of paper or other material used to decide something by chance

impeach: bring formal charges against a public official for crime or misconduct in office

J. MADISON   W. PATERSON

would be chosen by electors from each state, and he would serve four years. And yes, if it was necessary, he could be impeached.

But what if he should die while in office? Or be impeached? Who would take his place? So there had to be a vice president, the one who came in second in the presidential election. And since the vice president should do more than just wait around to see if the president would make it through his term, he was given the job of presiding over the Senate.

Mr. Randolph finished presenting his plan on May 29 and for the next two weeks—until June 13—the convention went over it. Some **measures** were voted on, some would be revised, and all would be discussed again and again. But there was also the chance that the whole plan would be scrapped for something else. After a day's recess, on June 15, William Paterson of New Jersey stood up. Only five feet two, he wasn't as impressive a figure as Mr. Randolph, but he was a cheerful, modest, likable man. Still, he didn't approve of a single idea of Mr. Randolph's.

The government should be a federation of states as it was now, with each state having an equal vote, he said. It should consist of one legislative body with several executives at its head.

measures: legislative acts or bills

According to Mr. Paterson, the Virginia Plan was impractical, illegal, and expensive. How could so many members of Congress, he asked, find the money to travel from all over the country to attend meetings?

When James Madison answered Mr. Paterson, it was as if he were fencing. Madison danced all around Mr. Paterson's arguments, **thrusting** at first one point, then another until it seemed as if there were nothing left of William Paterson's plan. And there wasn't. When the delegates were asked to vote in favor of one of the two plans, Mr. Randolph's won. Seven states against three. (Maryland's delegation was divided.) Randolph's plan still had to be thrashed out, but the idea of a federation was dead. With this vote the delegates committed themselves to write a constitution for a new nation, whether all of them were willing to call it that or not.

thrusting: forceful, sudden pushing

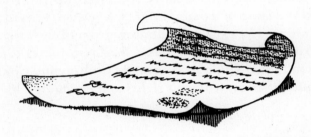

When the convention ended in September 1787, the Articles of Confederation were no more, and the new Constitution of the United States had been signed. The delegates had adopted in large part a new plan for government written by James Madison and presented at the convention by Edmund Randolph of Virginia. This plan would establish a republic with a national government consisting of three branches. Throughout the convention, the delegates made many compromises until they created a written plan of government that all could support. The Constitution and its amendments still serve as the basis of the government of the United States.

Source: Jean Fritz, *Shh! We're Writing the Constitution.* New York: G. P. Putnam's Sons, 1987.

Two Views on Women's Rights

by Abigail Adams and John Adams, 1776

In the spring of 1776, many Americans were expecting the 13 colonies to declare their independence from Britain. Once independence was achieved, some people hoped that the new government would treat women and men as equals under the law. One of these people was Abigail Adams (1744-1818), the 31-year-old wife of colonial leader John Adams (1735-1826). At the time, American women had few legal rights or powers. The Adamses were a close couple, and Abigail called John her "dearest friend" and "beloved partner." On the issue of women's rights, however, the Adamses had very different opinions. The excerpts below are from three letters that were written in 1776 while Abigail was in Massachusetts running the family farm and John was in Philadelphia serving in the Continental Congress. How do their views differ on women's rights and equality?

Abigail to John, March 31, 1776

I long to hear that you have declared **an independency**—and by the way in the new code of laws which I suppose it will be necessary for you to make I desire you would remember the ladies, and be more generous and favorable to them than your ancestors. Do not put such unlimited power into the hands of the husbands. Remember all men would be **tyrants** if they could. If particular care and attention is not paid to the ladies we are determined to **foment** a rebellion, and will not hold ourselves bound by any laws in which we have no voice, or representation.

That your sex are naturally tyrannical is a truth so thoroughly established as to **admit** of no **dispute**, but such of you as wish to be happy willingly give up the harsh title of master for the more tender and endearing one of friend. Why then, not put it out of the power of the vicious and the lawless to use us with cruelty and indignity. . . . Men of sense in all ages **abhor** those customs which treat us only as the **vassals** of your sex. Regard us then as beings placed by **providence** under your protection and in imitation of the Supreme Being make use of that power only for our happiness.

an independency: independence

tyrants: oppressive rulers

foment: stir up

admit: be
dispute: disagreement

abhor: hate
vassals: servants
providence: God

John to Abigail, April 14, 1776

As to Declarations of Independency, be patient. . . .

As to your extraordinary code of laws, I cannot but laugh. We have been told that our struggle has loosened the **bands** of government every where. That children and **apprentices** were disobedient—that schools and colleges were grown **turbulent**—that Indians **slighted** their guardians and Negroes grew **insolent** to their masters. But your letter was the first **intimation** that another tribe more numerous and powerful than all the rest were grown discontented. . . .

Depend upon it, we know better than to **repeal** our masculine systems. Although they are in full force, you know that they are little more than **theory**. We dare not exert our power in its full **latitude**. We are obliged to go fair, and softly, and in practice you know we are the **subjects**. We have only the name of masters, and rather than give up this, which would completely subject us to the **despotism** of the **petticoat**, I hope General Washington, and all our brave heroes would fight.

bands: ties

apprentices: workers learning a trade

turbulent: stormy
slighted: showed disrespect to
insolent: disrespectful
intimation: clue
repeal: undo

theory: unsure belief
latitude: strength
subjects: ones who obey

despotism: oppressive rule
petticoat: woman's skirt; old symbol for a woman

Abigail to John, May 7, 1776

I can not say that I think you very generous to the ladies, for whilst you are **proclaiming** peace and good will to men, **emancipating** all nations, you insist upon retaining an absolute power over wives. But you must remember that **arbitrary** power is like most other things which are very hard, very **liable** to be broken—and notwithstanding all your wise laws and **maxims** we have it in our power not only to free ourselves but to **subdue** our masters, and without violence throw both your natural and legal authority at our feet. . . .

proclaiming: announcing
emancipating: freeing

arbitrary: unlimited
liable: likely
maxims: truths
subdue: conquer

John Adams later served as second President of the United States from 1797 to 1801. His views of women's rights and equality were similar to those of most American men of his day. As First Lady, Abigail Adams assisted her husband in the White House. It would be many years, however, before women received the same rights as men.

Source: L. H. Butterfield, ed., *Adams Family Correspondence*, Vol. I. Cambridge, MA: The Belknap Press of Harvard University Press, 1963.

The Federalist, Number 10

by James Madison, 1787

By September 1787 the new Constitution of the United States was finished. It was now up to the states to ratify it. Opinion was divided between those who favored a strong central government, called Federalists, and those who favored more control by the states. One of the leading Federalists was James Madison. Madison and others wrote a series of unsigned letters to the newspapers in New York City arguing in favor of the Constitution. Below is an excerpt from one of these letters. Why do you think Madison did not sign the letters?

*T*he question resulting is whether small or extensive republics are most favorable to the election of proper guardians of the public **weal**; and it is clearly decided in favor of the latter by two obvious considerations:

weal: well-being

In the first place it is to be remarked that however small the republic may be the representatives must be raised to a certain number in order to guard against the **cabals** of a few; and that however large it may be they must be limited to a certain number in order to guard against the confusion of a **multitude**. . . .

cabals: secret plots

multitude: crowd

In the next place, as each representative will be chosen by a greater number of citizens in the large than in the small republic, it will be more difficult for unworthy candidates to practise with success the vicious arts by which elections are too often carried; and the **suffrages** of the people being more free, will be more likely to center on men who possess the most attractive merit and the most **diffusive** and established characters. . . .

suffrages: votes

diffusive: well-rounded

Extend the **sphere** and you take in a greater variety of parties and interests; you make it less probable that a majority of the whole will have a common motive to invade the rights of other citizens; or if such a common motive exists, it will be more difficult for all who feel it to discover their own strength and to act in unison with each other. . . .

sphere: a round object like a ball; here meaning the group of voters

The influence of **factious leaders** may **kindle** a flame within their particular States but will be unable to spread a general **conflagration** through the other States.

factious leaders: leaders who try to divide people from each other

kindle: start, as in a fire

conflagration: large, uncontrollable fire

The letters, numbering 85, sent between 1787 and 1788, have been called "the best commentary on the principles of government ever written." This statement was made by Thomas Jefferson, who did not support the Federalist position.

Source: Alexander Hamilton, James Madison, and John Jay, *The Federalist Papers.* New York: New American Library, 1961.

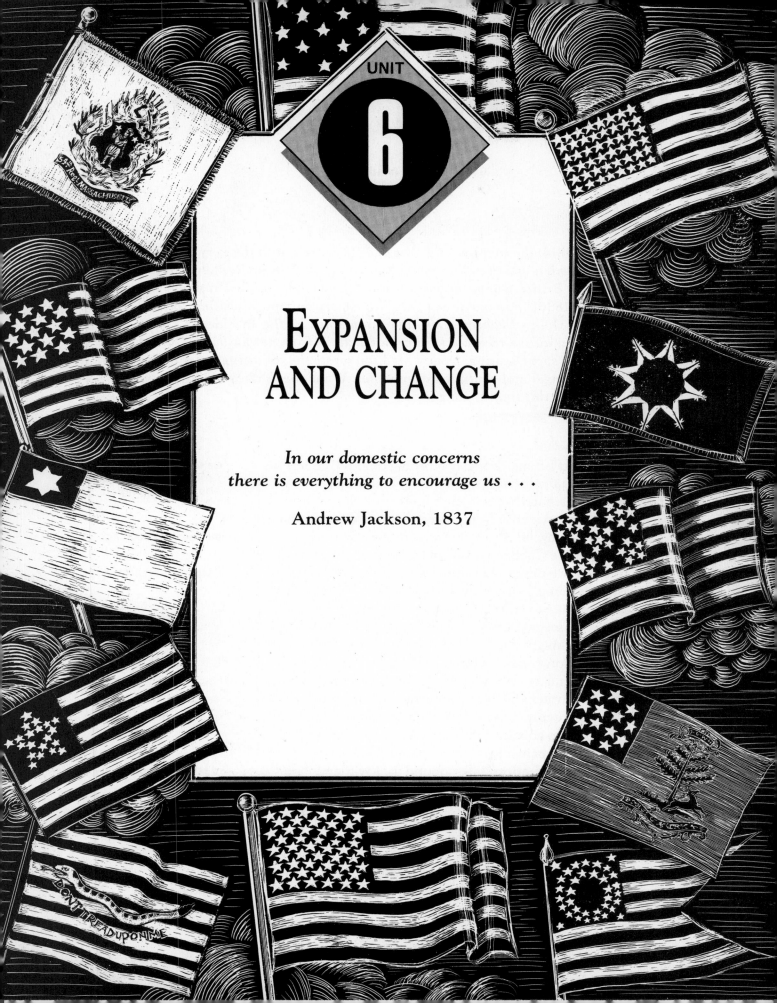

UNIT

6

EXPANSION
AND CHANGE

*In our domestic concerns
there is everything to encourage us . . .*

Andrew Jackson, 1837

Escape from Washington

by Dolley Madison, 1814

On August 23, 1814, the two-year-old War of 1812 moved onto the very doorstep of the White House, which was then known as the President's House. Residents of the city began fleeing as British troops marched toward the capital. While President James Madison (1751-1836) rode out to support the American troops waiting to fight the British, his wife Dolley Madison (1768-1849) remained in the President's House. She refused to leave until she received further instructions from her husband. During these long, tense hours spent waiting, Dolley Madison wrote the following letter to her sister, describing the danger and confusion around her. What does Dolley Madison consider her main duties in this time of danger?

Dear Sister,   *Tuesday, August 23, 1814*

My husband left me yesterday morning to join **General Winder.** He inquired anxiously whether I had courage or firmness to remain in the President's house until his return . . . and on my assurance that I had no fear but for him, and the success of our army, he left, **beseeching** me to take care of myself, and of the Cabinet papers, public and private. I have since received two **despatches** from him, written with a pencil. The last is alarming, because he desires I should be ready at a moment's warning to enter my carriage, and leave the city; that the enemy seemed stronger than had at first been reported, and it might happen that they would reach the city with the intention of destroying it. I am accordingly ready; I have pressed as many Cabinet papers into trunks as to fill one carriage; our private property must be **sacrificed,** as it is impossible to **procure** wagons for its transportation. I am determined not to go myself until I see Mr. Madison safe, so that he can accompany me, as I hear of much hostility towards him. **Disaffection** stalks around us. My friends and acquaintances are all gone. . . .

Wednesday Morning, August 24, 1814, twelve o'clock

Since sunrise I have been turning my spy-glass in every direction, and watching with unwearied anxiety, hoping to discover the approach of my dear husband and his friends; but, alas! I can **descry** only groups of military, wandering in all

General Winder: commander of troops outside Washington, D.C.

beseeching: begging

despatches: reports

sacrificed: given up
procure: get

disaffection: disloyalty

descry: spot

directions, as if there was a lack of **arms**, or of spirit to fight for their own fireside.

Three o'clock

Will you believe it, my sister? we have had a battle, or skirmish, near **Bladensburg**, and here I am still, within sound of the cannon! Mr. Madison comes not. May God protect us! Two messengers, covered with dust, come to bid me fly; but here I mean to wait for him. . . . At this late hour a wagon has been procured, and I have had it filled with **plate** and the most valuable **portable** articles, belonging to the house. Whether it will reach its destination . . . or fall into the hands of British soldiery, events must determine. Our kind friend, Mr. Carroll, has come to hasten my departure, and [is] in a very bad **humor** with me, because I insist on waiting until the large picture of General Washington is **secured**, and it requires to be unscrewed from the wall. This process was found too **tedious** for these **perilous** moments; I have ordered the frame to be broken, and the canvas taken out. It is done! and the precious portrait [is now] placed . . . for safe keeping. And now, dear sister, I must leave this house, or the retreating army will make me a prisoner in it by filling up the road I am directed to take. When I shall again write to you, or where I shall be tomorrow, I cannot tell!

arms: weapons

Bladensburg: Maryland town bordering Washington, D.C.

plate: costly dishes and silverware
portable: movable

humor: mood
secured: safe

tedious: long and difficult
perilous: dangerous

A few hours after Dolley Madison left Washington, D.C., on August 24, 1814, British soldiers marched in and set fire to the President's House and the rest of the city. Light from the enormous blaze could be seen 40 miles (64 km) away. Dolley Madison, dressed in the disguise of a poor country woman, escaped safely through the burning city to nearby Virginia. Several days later she returned to Washington and found much of the capital in ruins. Because the President's House had burned down, Dolley Madison and her husband had to live in a different house for the next two and a half years. When the President's House was rebuilt several years later, its outside walls were painted white. This is probably why it became known as the White House.

Source: *Memoirs and Letters of Dolley Madison, Wife of James Madison, President of the United States.* Boston: Houghton, Mifflin and Company, 1887.

The Journals of Lewis and Clark

Journal Entry by Meriwether Lewis, 1805

In 1803 at the request of President Thomas Jefferson, Meriwether Lewis and William Clark led an expedition to explore the land that the United States had just purchased from France, known as the Louisiana Territory. Their job included exploring the Missouri River and finding a safe passage west to the Pacific Ocean. President Jefferson asked them to write a description of everything they saw on their expedition. Why do you suppose President Jefferson wanted this? Below is a journal entry from their expedition.

August 12, 1805

We fell in with a large and plain Indian road, which came into the cove from the northeast and led along the foot of the mountains to the southwest, **obliquely** approaching the main stream, which we had left yesterday. This road we now pursued to the southwest. At 5 miles it passed a stout stream which is a principal fork of the main stream and falls into it just above the narrow pass between the two cliffs before mentioned, which we now saw below us. Here we halted and breakfasted on the last of our **venison**, having yet a small piece of pork in reserve. After eating, we continued our route through the low bottom of the main stream along the foot of the mountains on our right. The valley for 5 miles farther in a southwest direction was from 2 to 3 miles wide.

At the distance of 4 miles further, the road took us to the most distant fountain of the waters of the mighty Missouri in search of which we have spent so many **toilsome** days and restless nights. Thus far I had accomplished one of those great objects on which my mind has been unalterably fixed for many years. Judge, then, of the pleasure I felt in **allaying** my thirst with this pure and ice-cold water which issues from the base of a low mountain or hill of a gentle ascent for 1/2 a mile....Two miles below, McNeal had exultingly stood with a foot on each side of this little rivulet and thanked his God that he had lived to bestride the mighty, and heretofore deemed endless, Missouri.

After refreshing ourselves, we proceeded on to the top of the dividing ridge, from which I discovered immense ranges of high mountains still to the west of us, with their tops partially covered with snow. I now descended the mountain about 3/4 of a mile, which I found much steeper than on the opposite side, to a handsome bold running creek of cold, clear water. Here I first tasted the water of the great Columbia River.

obliquely: indirectly

venison: deer meat

toilsome: full of toil or work

allaying: relieving

The Lewis and Clark expedition left St. Louis, Missouri, in May 1803, and reached the Pacific Ocean in November 1805. Lewis and Clark mapped and explored over 3,000 miles of land, making it easier for new settlers to find their way west.

Source: John Bakeless, ed., *The Journals of Lewis and Clark.* New York: New American Library, 1964.

The Removal of the Cherokee

by John G. Burnett, 1890

During the 1830s many Cherokee and other Native Americans fought the Indian Removal Act, which ordered them to leave their homes in the southeastern United States. The Cherokee, who had their own constitution and government, took their case to the Supreme Court. The Court supported their right to the land, but President Andrew Jackson and his successor, Martin Van Buren, refused to follow the Court's decision. In 1838 the United States Army began to remove more than 15,000 Cherokee from their homeland by force. One of the soldiers in the army was John G. Burnett, a 27-year-old native of Tennessee who had grown up among the Cherokee. Over 50 years later, in 1890, Burnett wrote down his memories of this forced 800-mile (1,287-km) march of the Cherokee, which came to be known as the "Trail of Tears." As you read this excerpt, think about why Burnett might have written down what happened.

In the year of 1828, a little Indian boy living on Ward creek had sold a Gold nugget to a white trader, and that nugget sealed the doom of the Cherokees. In a short time the country was over run with armed **brigands** claiming to be Government Agents, who paid no attention to the rights of the Indians who were the legal possessors of the country. Crimes were committed that were a disgrace to civilization. Men were shot in cold blood, lands were **confiscated**. Homes were burned and the inhabitants driven out by these Gold hungry brigands. . . .

brigands: bandits

confiscated: taken away

Chief John Ross sent . . . an **envoy** to plead with President Jackson for protection for his people, but Jackson's manner was cold and indifferent. . . . "Sir [Jackson said] your audience is ended, there is nothing I can do for you." The doom of the Cherokee was sealed, Washington, D.C. had decreed that they must be driven West, and their lands given to the white man, and in May 1838 an Army of four thousand regulars, and three thousand volunteer soldiers . . . marched into the Indian country and wrote the blackest chapter on the pages of American History. . . .

Chief John Ross: leader of the Cherokee
envoy: representative

The removal of the Cherokee Indians from their life long homes in the year of 1838 found me . . . a Private soldier in the American Army. Being acquainted with many of the Indians and able to **fluently** speak their language, I was sent as interpreter into the **Smoky Mountain Country** in May, 1838, and witnessed the execution of the most brutal order in the History of American Warfare. I saw the helpless Cherokees arrested and dragged from their homes, and

fluently: easily
Smoky Mountain Country: mountain region of Georgia, North Carolina, and Tennessee

driven at the **bayonet** point into the **stockades**. And in the chill of a drizzling rain on an October morning I saw them loaded like cattle or sheep into six hundred and forty-five wagons and started toward the west.

One can never forget the sadness and **solemnity** of that [October] morning [in 1838]. Chief John Ross led in prayer and when the bugle sounded and the wagons started rolling many of the children rose to their feet and waved their little hands good-by to their mountain homes, knowing they were leaving them forever. Many of these helpless people did not have blankets and many of them had been driven from home barefooted.

On the morning of November the 17th we encountered a terrific sleet and snow storm with freezing temperatures and from that day until we reached the end of the fateful journey on March the 26th 1839, the sufferings of the Cherokees were awful. The trail of the **exiles** was a trail of death. They had to sleep in the wagons and on the ground without fire. And I have known as many as twenty-two of them to die in one night of pneumonia due to ill treatment, cold, and exposure. Among this number was the . . . wife of Chief John Ross. This noble hearted woman died a **martyr** to childhood, giving her only blanket for the protection of a sick child. She rode thinly clad through a blinding sleet and snow storm, developed pneumonia and died in the still hours of a bleak winter night, with her head resting on Lieutenant Gregg's saddle blanket. . . .

I was on guard duty the night Mrs. Ross died. When **relieved** at midnight I did not **retire**, but remained around the wagon out of sympathy for Chief Ross, and at daylight was **detailed** by Captain McClellan to assist in the burial. . . . Her uncoffined body was buried in a shallow grave by the roadside far from her native mountain home, and the sorrowing **Cavalcade** moved on. . . .

The long painful journey to the west ended March 26th, 1839, with four-thousand silent graves reaching from the foothills of the Smoky Mountains to what is known as Indian territory in the West. And **covetousness** on the part of the white race was the cause of all that the Cherokees had to suffer. . . .

School children of today do not know that we are living on lands that were taken . . . at the bayonet point to satisfy the white man's greed for gold. . . . Let the Historian of a future day tell the sad story with its sighs, its tears and dying groans.

Not all the Cherokee made this tragic trip. A few hundred managed to hide in the mountains of North Carolina and escape removal from their land. Today their descendants are known as the Eastern Cherokee. Those who survived the Trail of Tears settled in present-day Oklahoma. There the Cherokee and other Native Americans set up new homes and governments based on written constitutions. White settlers, however, soon began taking these lands just as they had in the Southeast. In the late 1800s many of the same Cherokee and other Native Americans would be forced out of Oklahoma.

Source: *Journal of Cherokee Studies*, Vol. 3, Summer 1978.

Glossary:

bayonet: steel blade on the tip of a rifle

stockades: military prisons

solemnity: seriousness

exiles: people forced from their country

martyr: person who suffers death for a cause

relieved: freed from duty

retire: go to bed

detailed: ordered

cavalcade: group of wagons

covetousness: greed, wanting another's possessions

Farewell Address

by Andrew Jackson, 1837

President Andrew Jackson believed that one way to end the tensions between Native Americans and white settlers in the Southeast was to relocate the Native Americans to lands west of the Mississippi River. Read the following excerpt from Jackson's farewell address to the American people. Why do you think President Jackson thought relocation was an acceptable idea?

We have now lived almost fifty years under the Constitution framed by the sages and patriots of the Revolution. The conflicts in which the nations of Europe were engaged during a great part of this period, the spirit in which they waged war against each other, and our **intimate commercial** connections with every part of the civilized world rendered it a time of much difficulty for the Government of the United States. We have had our seasons of peace and of war, with all the evils which precede or follow a state of hostility with powerful nations. We encountered these trials with our constitution yet in its infancy, and under the disadvantages which a new and untried government must always feel when it is called upon to put forth its whole strength without the lights of experience to guide it or the weight of **precedents** to justify its measures. But we have passed triumphantly through all these difficulties. Our Constitution is no longer a doubtful experiment, and at the end of nearly half a century we find that it has preserved **unimpaired** the liberties of the people, secured the rights of property, and that our country has improved and is flourishing beyond any former example in the history of nations.

In our domestic concerns there is everything to encourage us, and if you are true to yourselves nothing can **impede** your march to the highest point of national prosperity. The states which had so long been **retarded** in their improvement by the Indian tribes residing in the midst of them are at length relieved from the evil, and this unhappy race—the original dwellers in our land—are now placed in a situation where we may well hope that they will share in the blessings of civilization and be saved from that **degradation** and destruction to which they were rapidly hastening while they remained in the States; and while the safety and comfort of our own citizens have been greatly promoted by their removal, the **philanthropist** will rejoice that the remnant of that ill-fated race has been at length placed beyond the reach of injury or oppression, and that the **paternal** care of the General Government will hereafter watch over them and protect them.

intimate commercial: close business

precedents: prior examples

unimpaired: not lessened, whole, complete

impede: interrupt, delay, block

retarded: delayed, held back

degradation: lowering in quality

philanthropist: one who helps others

paternal: fatherly, parental

As you have read, in 1837 the United States government forced the Cherokee to relocate to the Indian Territory, which is now the state of Oklahoma.

Source: Francis Newton Thorpe, ed., *The Principles of American Statesmanship.* New York: Tandy-Thomas Company, 1909.

The Factory Bell

by an Unknown Factory Girl, 1844

The first large group of factory workers in the United States was made up of New England girls and women ranging in age from about 11 to 25. In the early and middle 1800s many left their small farms in the country for jobs in the mill towns. On the farm, the rising and setting of the sun and the changing of the seasons had determined which tasks people did each day. In the factory, however, all this changed. In mill towns across New England, daily life was suddenly shaped by clocks and bells that told workers when to wake, when to eat, when to work, and when to sleep. Look at the timetable of the Lowell Mills in Massachusetts printed on the next page. How might it have felt to live by such a strict schedule? To get an idea, read the poem below by an unknown factory girl. This poem first appeared on May 25, 1844, in the Factory Girl's Garland, a mill workers' newspaper in Exeter, New Hampshire. Why do you think the poet wrote a poem about bells?

Loud the morning bell is ringing,
  Up, up sleepers, haste away;
Yonder sits the redbreast singing,
  But to **list** we must not stay.

Not for us is morning breaking,
  Though we with **Aurora** rise;
Nor for us is Nature waking,
  All her smiles through earth and skies.

Sisters, haste, the bell is **tolling**,
  Soon will close the dreadful gate;
Then, alas! we must go strolling,
  Through the **counting-room**, too late.

Now the sun is upward climbing,
  And the breakfast hour has come;
Ding, dong, ding, the bell is chiming,
  Hasten, sisters, hasten home.

Quickly now we take our **ration**,
  For the bell will babble soon;
Each must hurry to her station,
  There to toil till weary noon.

Mid-day sun in heaven is shining,
  Merrily now the clear bell rings,
And the grateful hour of dining,
  To us weary sisters brings.

Now we give a welcome greeting,
  To these **viands** cooked so well;
Horrors! oh! not half done eating—
  Rattle, rattle goes the bell!

Sol behind the hills descended,
  Upward throws his ruby light;
Ding dong ding,—our toil is ended,
  Joyous bell, good night, good night.

list: listen
Aurora: dawn
tolling: ringing
counting-room: business room in the factory
ration: food
viands: meals
Sol: sun

TIME TABLE OF THE LOWELL MILLS,

Arranged to make the working time throughout the year average 11 hours per day.

TO TAKE EFFECT SEPTEMBER 21st., 1853.

The Standard time being that of the meridian of Lowell, as shown by the Regulator Clock of AMOS SANBORN, Post Office Corner, Central Street.

From March 20th to September 19th, inclusive.

COMMENCE WORK, at 6.30 A. M.   LEAVE OFF WORK, at 6.30 P. M., except on Saturday Evenings.
BREAKFAST at 6 A. M.   DINNER, at 12 M.   Commence Work, after dinner, 12.45 P. M.

From September 20th to March 19th, inclusive.

COMMENCE WORK at 7.00 A. M.   LEAVE OFF WORK, at 7.00 P. M., except on Saturday Evenings.
BREAKFAST at 6.30 A. M.   DINNER, at 12.30 P.M.   Commence Work, after dinner, 1.15 P. M.

BELLS.

From March 20th to September 19th, inclusive.

Morning Bells.	Dinner Bells.	Evening Bells.
First bell,..........4.30 A. M.	Ring out,..............12.00 M.	Ring out,............6.30 P. M.
Second, 5.30 A. M.; Third, 6.20.	Ring in,...........12.35 P. M.	Except on Saturday Evenings.

From September 20th to March 19th, inclusive.

Morning Bells.	Dinner Bells.	Evening Bells.
First bell,..........5.00 A. M.	Ring out,...........12.30 P. M.	Ring out at..........7.00 P. M.
Second, 6.00 A. M.; Third, 6.50.	Ring in,.............1.05 P. M.	Except on Saturday Evenings.

SATURDAY EVENING BELLS.

During APRIL, MAY, JUNE, JULY, and AUGUST, Ring Out, at 6.00 P. M.
The remaining Saturday Evenings in the year, ring out as follows :

SEPTEMBER.	NOVEMBER.	JANUARY.
First Saturday, ring out 6.00 P. M.	Third Saturday ring out 4.00 P. M.	Third Saturday, ring out 4.25 P. M.
Second " " 5.45 "	Fourth " " 3.55 "	Fourth " " 4.35 "
Third " " 5.30 "		
Fourth " " 5.20 "	**DECEMBER.**	**FEBRUARY.**

OCTOBER.		
	First Saturday, ring out 3.50 P. M.	First Saturday, ring out 4.45 P. M.
First Saturday, ring out 5.05 P. M.	Second " " 3.55 "	Second " " 4.55 "
Second " " 4.55 "	Third " " 3.55 "	Third " " 5.00 "
Third " " 4.45 "	Fourth " " 4.00 "	Fourth " " 5.10 "
Fourth " " 4.35 "	Fifth " " 4.00 "	
Fifth " " 4.25 "		**MARCH.**

NOVEMBER.	JANUARY.	
		First Saturday, ring out 5.25 P. M.
		Second " " 5.30 "
First Saturday, ring out 4.15 P. M.	First Saturday, ring out 4.10 P. M.	Third " " 5.35 "
Second ". " 4.05 "	Second " " 4.15 "	Fourth " " 5.45 "

YARD GATES will be opened at the first stroke of the bells for entering or leaving the Mills.

•°   *SPEED GATES commence hoisting three minutes before commencing work.*

During the 1800s factory towns like Lowell, Massachusetts, and Exeter, New Hampshire, began growing throughout the United States. More and more Americans began to live according to clocks, rather than the sun, as they took jobs in new factories and cities. Today it is hard for most Americans to think of living without clocks. How much does your own life revolve around clocks and bells? Imagine living without them. How would your life be different?

Source: *Factory Girl's Garland*, May 25, 1844, reprinted in Philip S. Foner, ed., *The Factory Girls*. Urbana, IL: University of Illinois Press, 1977.

Last Appeal for Aid

by William Travis, 1836

By the middle 1800s large numbers of Americans had settled in Texas, which was then part of Mexico. As their numbers grew, talk of independence became widespread. Such talk alarmed President Santa Anna of Mexico, and soon he and his army were on the march into Texas. In December 1835 pro-independence forces, under the leadership of William Travis, took control of the Alamo. The Alamo was an old Spanish mission in San Antonio that had been turned into a fort. Below is an excerpt from Travis's last appeal to the United States government for more help for his small army of 200 at the Alamo. Why were the Texans at the Alamo prepared to defend it to the death?

March 3, 1836

*S*ir,— . . . I beg leave to communicate to you the situation of this **garrison**. You have doubtless already seen my official report of the action . . . to Gen. Sam. Houston, together with the various communications **heretofore** sent by express. I shall therefore **confine** myself to what has **transpired** since that date. . . . The spirits of my men are still high, although they have had much to depress them. We have **contended** for ten days against an enemy whose numbers are variously estimated at from fifteen hundred to six thousand men. I hope your honourable body will hasten on reinforcements, ammunition, and **provisions** to our aid, as soon as possible. We have provisions for twenty days for the men we have— our supply of ammunition is limited. . . .

If these things are promptly sent and large reinforcements are hastened to this frontier, this neighborhood will be the great and decisive battle ground. The power of Santa Anna is to be met here, or in the colonies; we had better meet them here, than to suffer a war of desolation to rage in our settlements. . . . They have declared us [rebels] and demanded that we should surrender **at discretion**, or that this garrison should **be put to the sword**. Their threats have had no influence on me, or my men, but to make all fight with desperation, and that high souled courage which characterizes the patriot, who is willing to die in defence of his country's liberty and his own honor. . . .

The bearer of this will give your honorable body a statement more in detail, should he escape through the enemy's lines—God and Texas—*Victory or Death!*

P.S. The enemy's troops are still arriving, and the reinforcement will probably amount to two or three thousand.

garrison: military post

heretofore: before this time

confine: limit

transpired: happened

contended: fought

provisions: supplies

at discretion: on their (in this case, the Mexican army's) terms

be put to the sword: executed

On March 6, 1836, the Alamo fell to the Mexican army. All of the Texans lost their lives in this battle. "Remember the Alamo!" became the rallying cry in the Texas fight for independence.

Source: Ernest Wallace, David M. Vigness, and George B. Ward, eds., *Documents of Texas History.* Austin: State House Press, 1994.

ERIE CANAL

Traditional Song, 1800s

When the Erie Canal opened in 1825, it became one of the busiest transportation routes in the United States. The canal carried travelers and goods between Albany and Buffalo in New York State. As they labored, canal workers made up songs describing their lives, their jobs, and even the mules that towed the boats under very low bridges by walking on paths alongside the canal. What does the following song tell you about working on the Erie Canal?

I got a mule, her name is Sal, Fif-teen miles on the

E-rie Ca-nal!__ She's a good old work-er and a good old pal,

Fif-teen miles on the E-rie Ca-nal!__ We've hauled some barg-es

in our day, Filled with lum-ber, coal and hay, And we know ev'-ry

inch of the way From Al-ba-ny__ to__ Buf-fa-lo.__

Low bridge, ev-'ry-bod-y down, Low bridge, 'cause we're com-ing to a town;

And you'll al-ways know your neigh-bor, You'll al-ways know your pal,

If you ev-er nav-i-gat-ed on the E-rie Ca-nal.__

Source: *Music and You*. New York: Macmillan Publishing Company, 1988.

SWEET BETSY FROM PIKE

Traditional Song, 1800s

In 1849, soon after the discovery of gold in California, thousands of people rushed to the Sierra Nevada mountains, hoping to strike it rich. As many of these "Forty-Niners" bumped along in their covered wagons, they sang songs to help them pass the time. The song below was one of their favorites. What parts of the song do you think held a special meaning for those traveling west?

Adapted by Merrill Staton

1. Oh, do you re-mem-ber sweet Bet-sy from Pike, Who crossed the wide prai-ries with her broth-er Ike? With two yoke of ox-en, a big yal-ler dog, A tall Shang-hai roos-ter, and one spot-ted hog.

Refrain

Hoo-dle dang, fol-de-dye-do, hoo-dle dang, fol-de-day. Hoo-dle dang, fol-de dye-do, hoo-dle dang, fol-de-day.

2. They soon reached the desert where Betsy gave out,
   And down in the sand she lay rollin' about.
   When Ike saw sweet Betsy he said with surprise,
   "You'd better get up, you'll get sand in your eyes." *Refrain*

3. Said Ike, "Ole Pike County, I'll go back to you,"
   Said Betsy, "You'll go by yourself if you do,
   There's no time for pleasure and no time for rest,
   In spite of our troubles we'll keep headin' west." *Refrain*

4. They camped on the prairie for weeks upon weeks.
   They swam the wide rivers and crossed the tall peaks.
   And soon they were rollin' in nuggets of gold.
   You may not believe it but that's what we're told. *Refrain*

Source: *Music and You.* New York: Macmillan Publishing Company, 1988.

Diary of an Overland Journey to California

by Sallie Hester, 1849

During the middle 1800s up to half a million people made the rugged overland journey to California and Oregon. Among them were 12-year-old Sallie Hester and her family from Indiana. Like many pioneers, Sallie kept a diary of her seven-month, westward journey across the continent in 1849. As you read excerpts of Sallie's diary, think of the adventures she experienced and the hardships she faced. What type of skills and personal qualities would it have taken to survive this journey?

Bloomington, Indiana, March 20, 1849. Our family, consisting of father, mother, two brothers and one sister, left this morning for that far and much talked of country, California. Our **train** numbered fifty wagons. The last hours were spent in bidding goodby to old friends. My mother is heartbroken over this separation of relatives and friends. . . . The last goodby has been said, the last glimpse of our old home on the hill, and wave of hand at the old **Academy** with a goodby to kind teachers and schoolmates, and we are off.

train: traveling group

academy: school

New Albany, March 24. This is my first experience of a big city. We have been several days reaching it on account of the terrible conditions of the roads. Our carriage **upset** at one place. All were thrown out but no one was hurt. My mother thought it a bad **omen** and wanted to give up the trip.

upset: overturned
omen: sign

March 26. Took the steamboat *Meteor* this evening for **St. Joe.** Now sailing on the broad Ohio [River], toward the far west.

St. Joe: St. Joseph, Missouri

St. Joe, April 27. Here we are at last, safe and sound, laying in supplies and waiting our turn to be ferried across the river. As far as the eye can reach, so great is the **emigration**, you see nothing but wagons. This town presents a striking appearance — a vast army on wheels — crowds of men, women, and lots of children, and last but not least the cattle and horses upon which our lives will depend.

emigration: number of people moving

May 21. Camped on the beautiful [**Big**] **Blue River**, 215 miles [346 km] from St. Joe, with plenty of wood and water and good grazing for cattle. . . . We had two deaths in our train within the past week of **cholera** — young men going west to seek their fortunes. We buried them on the banks of the Blue River, far from home and friends.

Big Blue River: river in southeastern Nebraska

cholera: a deadly disease

We are now in the Pawnee Nation. . . . When we camp at night we form a **corral** with our wagons and pitch our tents on the outside, and inside of this corral we drive our cattle, with guards stationed on the outside of the tents.

corral: circle

We have a cooking stove made of sheet iron, a **portable** table, tin plates and cups, cheap knives and forks (best ones packed away) and camp stools. We sleep in our wagons on feather beds. The men who drive for us sleep in the tent. We live on bacon, ham, rice, dried fruits, molasses, packed butter, bread, coffee, tea and milk as we have our own cows. Occasionally the men kill an antelope and then we have a feast; and sometimes we have fish on Sunday.

portable: movable

June 3. Our tent is now pitched on the beautiful **Platte River**, 315 miles [507 km] from St. Joe. The cholera is raging. A great many deaths. Graves everywhere. We [my family] are all in good health. **Game** is scarce; a few antelope in sight. Roads bad.

Platte River: river in central Nebraska

game: animals hunted for food

Fort Laramie, Wyoming, June 19. This fort is of **adobe**, enclosed with a high wall. The entrance is a hole in the wall just large enough for a person to crawl through. The impression you have on entering is that you are in a small town. Men are engaged in all kinds of business from blacksmith up. We camped a mile from the fort, where we remained a few days to wash and **lighten up**.

adobe: bricks made of dried earth

lighten up: relax

struck: arrived at

June 21. Started over sixty miles [97 km] of the worst road in the world. Have again **struck** the Platte [River] and followed it until we came to the ferry. We had a great deal of trouble swimming our cattle across [and] taking our wagons to pieces. . . . A number of accidents happened here. A lady and four children were drowned through the carelessness of those in charge of the ferry.

July 2. Passed **Independence Rock**. This rock is covered with names. With great difficulty I found a place to cut mine. . . .

During the week we went over the South Pass and the **summit** of the Rocky Mountains.

Independence Rock: stone landmark in central Wyoming on which pioneers carved their names when they passed by

summit: peak

July 4. Had the pleasure of eating ice. . . . Had neither wood nor water for fifty-two miles [84 km]. Traveled in the night. At the

SALLIE HESTER'S ROUTE WEST, 1849

······· Sallie Hester's route
● City or town
⛺ Fort
)(Mountain pass
■ Landmark

Green River we lay by two days to rest man and beast after our long and weary journey.

August 18. This week some of our company left us, all young men. They were jolly, merry fellows and gave life to our lonely evenings. We all miss them very much. Some had violins, others guitars, and some had fine voices. They were anxious to hurry on without the Sunday stops. Roads are rocky and trying to our wagons, and the dust is horrible. The men wear veils tied over their hats as a protection. When we reach camp at night they are covered with dust from head to heels.

Humboldt River, August 20. We are now 348 miles [560 km] from the [gold] mines. We expect to travel that distance in three weeks and a half. Water and grass scarce. Though the water is not fit to drink— **slough** water—we are obliged to use it for it's all we have.

September 7. Stopped and cut grass for the cattle and supplied ourselves with water for the desert. Had a **trying** time crossing it. Several of our cattle gave out and we left one. Our journey through the desert was from Monday, three o'clock in the afternoon, until Thursday morning at sunrise. The weary journey that last night, the mooing of the cattle for water, the cry, "Another ox down," the

Green River: river in southwestern Wyoming

Humboldt River: river in northern Nevada

slough: swamp

trying: hard

stopping of the train to **unyoke** the poor dying **brute**, to let him follow at will or stop by the wayside and die, and the weary, weary tramp of men and beasts, worn out with heat and **famished** for water, will never be erased from my memory. Just at dawn in the distance we had a glimpse of the **Truckee River**, and with it the feeling: Saved at last! Poor cattle; they kept on mooing even when they stood knee deep in water. The long, dreaded desert has been crossed and we are all safe and well. Grass green and beautiful, and the cattle are up to their eyes in it.

September 11. Made eighteen miles [29 km]. Crossed Truckee River ten times. Came near being drowned at one of the crossings. Got frightened and jumped out of the carriage into the water. The current was very swift and carried me some distance down the stream. In jumping I expected to reach the shore; instead I landed in the water, but was rescued in time all right.

September 14. It was night when we crossed the summit of the **Sierra Nevada**, and I shall never forget our descent to the place where we are now encamped— our **tedious** march with pine **knots** blazing in the darkness and the tall, majestic pines towering above our heads. The scene was grand and gloomy beyond description. We could not ride—roads too narrow and rocky. It was a footsore and weary crowd that reached this camp.

September 21. Reached Bear Valley by descending a tremendous hill. We let the wagons down with ropes. Left one of our wagons and the springs of our carriage. Cut down trees for our cattle to **browse** on.

Vernon, California, October 6. Well, after a five-months trip from St. Joe, Missouri, our party of fifty wagons, now only thirteen, has at last reached this **haven** of rest. Strangers in a strange land, what will our future be?

Fremont, October 10. This is a small town on the opposite side of the river from Vernon. My father has decided to remain here for the winter. We have had a small house put up of two rooms made of boards with **puncheon** floor.

April 27 [1850]. Have met a number of nice young men here. I am too young for **beaux**, but the young men don't seem to think so.

unyoke: free
brute: animal
famished: dying of thirst

Truckee River: river in northwestern Nevada

Sierra Nevada: mountain range in California and Nevada
tedious: tiring
knots: branches

browse: graze

Vernon: town near San Francisco
haven: peaceful place

puncheon: split log

beaux (bōz): boyfriends

Despite the attention that she received from young men upon her arrival in California in 1849, Sallie chose not to get married until 1871, when she was 34 years old. By that time, just 22 years after Sallie's seven-month journey from Indiana, people could travel across the entire country to California by train—a trip that took only six days!

Source: Josef and Dorothy Berger, *Small Voices*. New York: Paul S. Eriksson, Inc., 1966.

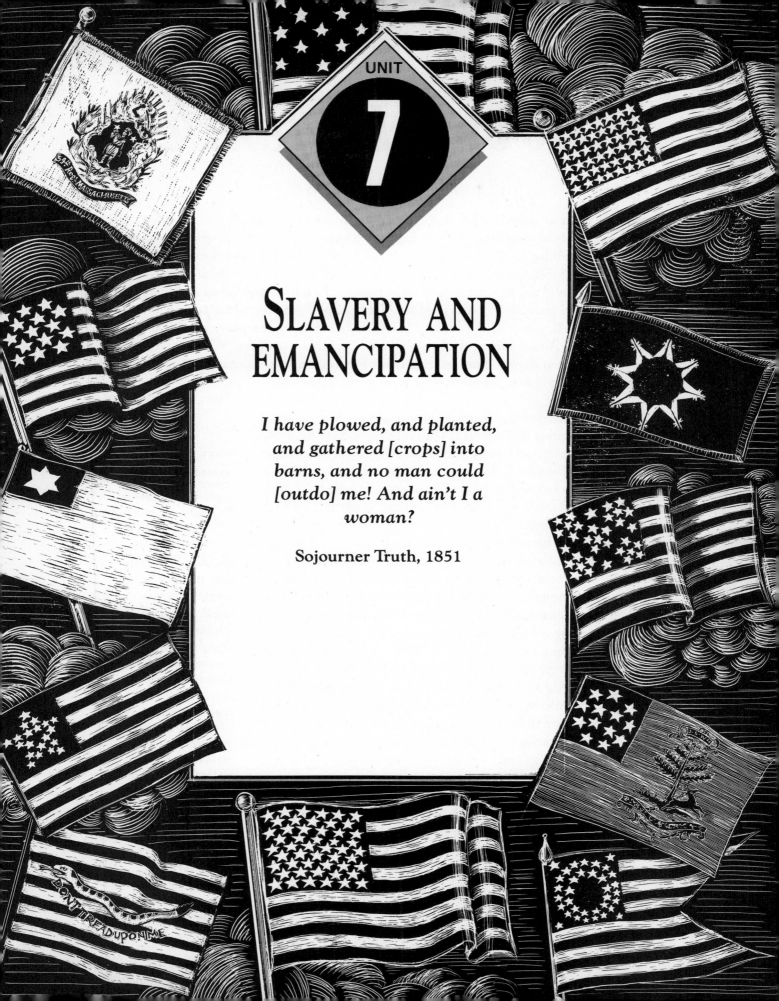

SLAVERY AND EMANCIPATION

I have plowed, and planted, and gathered [crops] into barns, and no man could [outdo] me! And ain't I a woman?

Sojourner Truth, 1851

Slavery Defended

by George Fitzhugh, 1857

Was slavery right or wrong? Although today the answer seems clear to us, in the 1800s Americans disagreed strongly with one another. Many people in the North felt slavery was evil. Many white Southerners, on the other hand, defended slavery and believed it was right. George Fitzhugh (1806–1881), a lawyer and slave owner from Port Royal, Virginia, was one of the fiercest defenders of slavery. In a book published in 1857, Fitzhugh claimed that slavery was good for black people, good for white people, and good for the country. As you read the excerpt below, notice how he compares the life of enslaved African Americans to the life of free white factory workers. What differences does he see between them? After reading what Fitzhugh wrote, compare his account with Frederick Douglass's description of slavery on pages 103–104.

The negro slaves of the South are the happiest, and, in some sense, the freest people in the world. The children and the aged and **infirm** work not at all, and yet have all the comforts and **necessaries** of life provided for them. They enjoy liberty, because they are **oppressed** neither by care nor labor. The women do little hard work, and are protected from the **despotism** of their husbands by their **masters.** The negro men and stout boys work, on the average, in good weather, not more than nine hours a day. The balance of their time is spent in perfect **abandon.** Besides, they have their **Sabbaths** and holidays. White men, with so much of **license** and liberty, would die of **ennui**; but negroes **luxuriate in corporeal** and mental **repose.** With their faces upturned to the sun, they can sleep at any hour. . . . [This sleep] results from contentment with the present, and confident **assurance** of the future. We do not know whether free laborers [in the North] ever sleep. They are fools to do so; for, whilst they sleep, the **wily** and watchful **capitalist** is devising means to **ensnare** and **exploitate** them. The free laborer must work or starve. He is more of a slave than the negro, because he works longer and harder for less **allowance** than the slave, and has no holiday, because the cares of life with him begin when its labors end. He has no liberty, and not a single right. . . .

Free laborers have not a thousandth part of the rights and liberties of negro slaves. Indeed, they have not a single right or a single liberty, unless it be the right or liberty to die.

infirm: sick

necessaries: needed items

oppressed: burdened

despotism: cruel misuse of power

masters: owners

abandon: relaxation

Sabbaths: Sundays

license: freedom

ennui: boredom

luxuriate in: enjoy totally

corporeal: physical

repose: rest

assurance: certainty

wily: clever

capitalist: business or factory owner

ensnare: trap

exploitate: misuse

allowance: reward

Many Southerners agreed with Fitzhugh. They believed that slavery was fair and that enslaved African Americans lived comfortable lives.

Source: George Fitzhugh, *Cannibals All! or, Slaves Without Masters*. Richmond, VA: Adolphus Morris, 1857.

Slavery Denounced

by Frederick Douglass, 1852

No person in the United States spoke out more forcefully against slavery than Frederick Douglass (1817–1895). Born into slavery in Maryland, Douglass escaped to New England in 1838. He became an abolitionist in the 1840s and began touring the North to denounce, or condemn, slavery. He settled in Rochester, New York, and started the North Star, an antislavery newspaper. In 1852 the people of Rochester asked Douglass to give a speech in honor of the Fourth of July. They expected him to speak about Independence Day and the greatness of the United States. But Douglass had a different message—one that shocked his listeners. As you read this excerpt from Douglass's Fourth of July speech, keep in mind the account of George Fitzhugh that you read on page 102. How does Douglass's argument concerning slavery and the equality of African Americans compare with Fitzhugh's? How does he argue for the rights and accomplishments of African Americans?

Fellow Citizens—Pardon me, and allow me to ask, why am I called upon to speak here today? What have I, or those I represent, to do with your national independence? Are the great **principles** of political freedom and of natural justice, **embodied** in that Declaration of Independence, extended to us? . . .

principles: ideas
embodied: contained

Such is not the state of the case. I say it with a sad sense of the **disparity** between us. I am not included within the **pale** of this glorious anniversary! Your high independence only reveals the immeasurable distance between us. The blessings in which you this day rejoice, are not enjoyed **in common**. The rich inheritance of justice, liberty, prosperity, and independence, **bequeathed** by your fathers, is shared by you, not by me. The sunlight that brought life and healing to you, has brought **stripes** and death to me. This Fourth of July is *yours*, not *mine*. *You* may rejoice, *I* must mourn. . . .

disparity: difference
pale: boundary

in common: by all
bequeathed: handed down

stripes: whippings

Fellow-citizens, above your national, **tumultuous** joy, I hear the mournful wail of millions, whose chains, heavy and **grievous** yesterday, are to-day **rendered** more **intolerable** by the **jubilant** shouts that reach them. If I do forget, if I do not faithfully remember those bleeding children of sorrow this day, "may . . . my tongue **cleave** to the roof of my mouth!" . . . My subject, then, fellow-citizens, is AMERICAN SLAVERY. I shall see this day and its popular **characteristics** from the slave's point of view. Standing there, identified with the American **bondman**, making his wrongs mine, I do not hesitate to declare, with all my soul, that the character and conduct of this nation never looked blacker to me than on this Fourth of July. Whether we turn to the declarations of the past, or to the **professions** of the present, the conduct of the nation seems

tumultuous: excited
grievous: painful
rendered: made
intolerable: unbearable
jubilant: joyful

cleave: stick

characteristics: features
bondman: slave

professions: beliefs

equally hideous and revolting. America is false to the past, false to the present, and solemnly **binds** herself to be false to the future. Standing with God and the crushed and bleeding slave on this occasion, I will . . . **denounce**, with all the emphasis I can command, everything that serves to **perpetuate** slavery—the great sin and shame of America! . . .

binds: promises

denounce: attack
perpetuate: continue

For the present, it is enough to **affirm** the equal manhood of the Negro race. Is it not astonishing that, while we are plowing, planting, and reaping, using all kinds of mechanical tools, erecting houses, constructing bridges, building ships, working in metals of brass, iron, copper, silver, and gold; that, while we are reading, writing, and **cyphering**, acting as clerks, merchants, and secretaries, having among us lawyers, doctors, ministers, poets, authors, editors, **orators**, and teachers; that, while we are engaged in all manner of **enterprises** common to other men—digging gold in California, capturing the whale in the Pacific, feeding sheep and cattle on the hillside, living, moving, acting, thinking, planning, living in families as husbands, wives, and children, and, above all, **confessing** and worshiping the Christian's God, and looking hopefully for life and **immortality** beyond the grave,—we are called upon to prove that we are men! . . .

affirm: declare

cyphering: doing mathematics

orators: speakers
enterprises: businesses

confessing: believing in

immortality: life after death

What! am I to argue that it is wrong to make men **brutes,** to rob them of their liberty, to work them without wages, to keep them **ignorant** of their relations to their fellow-men, to beat them with sticks, to **flay** their flesh with the **lash,** to load their limbs with irons, to hunt them with dogs, to sell them at auction, to **sunder** their families, to knock out their teeth, to burn their flesh, to starve them into obedience and submission to their masters? Must I argue that a system, thus marked with blood and stained with pollution, is wrong? No; I will not. I have better **employment** for my time. . . .

brutes: animals

ignorant: unaware
flay: strip away
lash: whip
sunder: break apart

employment: use

What to the American slave is your Fourth of July? I answer, a day that reveals to him, more than all other days in the year, the **gross** injustice and cruelty to which he is the constant victim. To him, your celebration is a **sham**; . . . your sounds of rejoicing are empty and heartless; . . . your shouts of liberty and equality [are] hollow mockery; your prayers and hymns . . . are to him mere . . . **fraud** . . . and hypocrisy—a thin veil to cover up crimes which would disgrace a nation of savages. There is not a nation on the earth guilty of practices more shocking and bloody, than are the people of these United States, at this very hour.

gross: outright
sham: fake

fraud: dishonesty

Frederick Douglass's speech in 1852 made clear that Americans had a long way to go to live up to the ideals of liberty and equality expressed in the Declaration of Independence. The powerful words of Douglass and other abolitionists helped convince many people of the evils of slavery.

Source: Frederick Douglass, *My Bondage and My Freedom*. New York and Auburn: Miller, Orton & Mulligan, 1855.

Follow the Drinking Gourd

Spiritual, 1800s

Enslaved people often expressed their pain and sorrow, hopes and dreams, in song. They also used music as a kind of code for communicating with one another. Perhaps no other song has served this urgent purpose so well as "Follow the Drinking Gourd." In the years leading up to and through the Civil War, slaves passed this song along from plantation to plantation. No ordinary set of lyrics, the words to the song told slaves how to travel through the countryside to reach the free North. The Big Dipper, or Drinking Gourd, pointed the way north. The three rivers mentioned in the song were the Tombigbee, the Tennessee, and the Ohio. The old man in the song was Peg Leg Joe, a white sailor who ferried escaping people across the river. Can you guess to what season the phrase "When the sun comes back and the first quail calls" refers?

Adapted by Paul Campbell

Verse
mp

1. When the sun comes back and the first quail calls,_____
2. Now the riv-er bank-'ll make___ a might-y good road;___ The
3. Now the riv - er ends___ be - tween two hills;___

Fol - low_____ the Drink - in' Gourd.___ Then the
dead trees - 'll show you the way. And the
Fol - low_____ the Drink - in' Gourd.___ And___

The Abolitionist cause, furthered by brave people like Harriet Tubman, Levi and Catherine Coffin, Frederick Douglass, and Sojourner Truth, came to a head during the middle 1800s. Still, for many years to come, the movement for equal rights for African Americans faced serious opposition. This struggle has given birth to many songs and other works of art. Can you think of any poems, paintings, books, movies, or other songs that deal with this subject?

Source: Adapted from *Share the Music, Book 6*. New York: Macmillan/McGraw-Hill, 1995.

Declaration of Sentiments and Resolutions

Declaration of the Seneca Falls Convention, 1848

Women's rights, like those of African Americans, were won slowly and painfully. In 1848 Lucretia Mott and Elizabeth Cady Stanton organized the first women's rights convention, which was held in Seneca Falls, New York. At this convention, the participants drafted a declaration that echoed the Declaration of Independence. Below is an excerpt from their Declaration of Sentiments and Resolutions, which is also known as the Declaration of Rights and Sentiments. What basic rights did these women seek?

When, in the course of human events, it becomes necessary for one portion of the family of man to assume among the people of the earth a position different from that which they have hitherto occupied, but one to which the laws of nature and of nature's God entitle them, a decent respect to the opinions of mankind requires that they should declare the causes that impel them to such a course.

We hold these truths to be self-evident: that all men and women are created equal; that they are endowed by their Creator with certain **inalienable** rights; that among these are life, liberty, and the pursuit of happiness; that to secure these rights governments are instituted, **deriving** their just powers from the consent of the governed. Whenever any form of government becomes destructive of these ends, it is the right of those who suffer from it to refuse allegiance to it. . . .

inalienable: can't be taken away

deriving: getting

The history of mankind is a history of repeated injuries and **usurpations** on the part of man toward woman, having in direct object the establishment of an absolute tyranny over her. To prove this, let facts be submitted to a candid world.

usurpations: taking over by force

He has never permitted her to exercise her inalienable right to the **elective franchise**.

He has compelled her to submit to laws, in the formation of which she had no voice.

elective franchise: right to vote

He has withheld from her rights which are given to the most ignorant and degraded men—both natives and foreigners.

Having deprived her of this first right of a citizen, the elective franchise, thereby leaving her without representation in the halls of legislation, he has oppressed her on all sides.

He has made her, if married, in the eye of the law, **civilly dead**.

civilly dead: without rights

He has taken from her all right in property, even to the wages she earns.

He has made her, morally, an irresponsible being, as she can commit many crimes with **impunity**, provided they be done in the presence of her husband. In the **covenant** of marriage, she is

impunity: without punishment
covenant: agreement, contract

compelled to promise obedience to her husband, he becoming, to all intents and purposes, her master—the law giving him power to deprive her of her liberty, and to **administer chastisement**.

adminster chastisement: punish

He has so framed the laws of divorce, as to what shall be the proper causes, and in case of separation, to whom the guardianship of the children shall be given, as to be wholly regardless of the happiness of women—the law, in all cases, going upon the false **supposition** of the supremacy of man, and giving all power into his hands.

supposition: belief

After depriving her of all rights as a married woman, if single, and the owner of property, he has taxed her to support a government which recognizes her only when her property can be made profitable to it.

He has monopolized nearly all the profitable employments, and from those she is permitted to follow, she receives but a **scanty remuneration**. He closes against her all the avenues to wealth and distinction which he considers most honorable to himself. As a teacher of **theology**, medicine, or law, she is not known.

scanty remuneration: small payment

theology: religion

He has denied her the facilities for obtaining a thorough education, all colleges being closed against her.

He allows her in Church, as well as State, but a subordinate position, claiming **Apostolic** authority for her exclusion from the ministry, and, with some exceptions, from any public participation in the affairs of the Church.

Apostolic: from the Apostles, or immediate followers, of Jesus

He has created a false public sentiment by giving to the world a different code of morals for men and women, by which moral **delinquencies** which exclude women from society, are not only tolerated, but deemed of little account in man.

delinquencies: failings

He has **usurped** the **prerogative** of **Jehovah** himself, claiming it as his right to assign for her a sphere of action, when that belongs to her conscience and to her God.

usurped: taken over
prerogative: sole right
Jehovah: Hebrew word for God

He has **endeavored**, in every way that he could, to destroy her confidence in her own powers, to lessen her self-respect, and to make her willing to lead a dependent and abject life.

endeavored: tried

Now, in view of this entire **disfranchisement** of one-half the people of this country, their social and religious degradation—in view of the unjust laws above mentioned, and because women do feel themselves aggrieved, oppressed, and **fraudulently** deprived of their most sacred rights, we insist that they have immediate admission to all the rights and privileges which belong to them as citizens of the United States.

disfranchisement: taking away of rights

fraudulently: falsely

Other leaders such as Susan B. Anthony, Carrie Chapman Catt, and Lucy Stone also fought for equal rights for women. Although Wyoming women were granted the right to vote in 1869, it wasn't until 1920 that American women gained the freedom to vote in elections at all levels of government.

Source: Diane Ravitch, ed., *The American Reader: Words That Moved a Nation.* New York: HarperCollins Publishers, 1990.

"Ain't I a Woman?"

by Sojourner Truth, 1851

Like Frederick Douglass, whose speech you read on pages 103–104, Sojourner Truth (1797?–1883) was one of the country's leading abolitionists. She also fought strongly for the rights of women. Enslaved in New York State for the first 30 years of her life, Sojourner Truth was freed in 1827. She became a preacher and a speaker and published her autobiography (which is shown on page 110) in 1850. One year later she attended a women's rights meeting in Akron, Ohio. As some men in the audience jeered one of the speakers, Truth suddenly stood up and began talking. The meeting's leader, Frances D. Gage, later wrote down Truth's unplanned speech. In her speech how does Sojourner Truth connect the rights of African Americans to the rights of women?

*W*ell, children, where there is so much racket there must be something out of **kilter**. I think that **'twixt** the Negroes of the South and the women of the North, all talking about rights, the white men will be in a fix pretty soon. But what's all this here talking about?

> **kilter:** place
> **'twixt:** between

That man over there says that women need to be helped into carriages, and lifted over ditches, and to have the best place everywhere. Nobody ever helps me into carriages, or over mud-puddles, or gives me any best place! And ain't I a woman? Look at me! Look at my arm! I have plowed, and planted, and gathered [crops] into barns, and no man could **head** me! And ain't I a woman? I could work as much and eat as much as a man—when I could get it—and bear the **lash** as well! And ain't I a woman? I have **borne** thirteen children, and seen them most all sold off to slavery, and when I cried out with my mother's grief, none but Jesus heard me! And ain't I a woman?

> **head:** outdo
>
> **lash:** whip
> **borne:** given birth to

Then they talk about this thing in the head; what's this they call it? (**"Intellect,"** whispered someone near.) That's it, honey. What's that got to do with women's rights or Negroes' rights? If my cup won't hold but a **pint**, and yours holds a quart, wouldn't you be mean not to let me have my little half-measure full?

> **intellect:** ability to think
>
> **pint:** half-quart

Then that little man in black there, he says women can't have as much rights as men, because Christ wasn't a woman! Where did your Christ come from? Where did your Christ come from? From God and a woman! Man had nothing to do with Him.

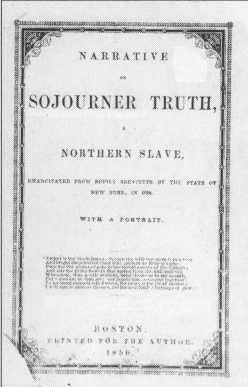

If the first woman God ever made was strong enough to turn the world upside down all alone, these women together ought to be able to turn it back, and get it right side up again! And now that they are asking to do it, the men had better let them.

Obliged to you for hearing me, and now old Sojourner hasn't got anything more to say.

obliged: many thanks

When Sojourner Truth finished speaking, the audience roared its approval. Truth went on to speak at many other meetings around the country. She was not always welcomed. In Kansas she was clubbed, and in Missouri she was attacked by a mob, yet Truth continued to speak out bravely for the rights of both African Americans and women. During the 1840s and 1850s women abolitionists such as Sojourner Truth helped to make freedom and equal rights for all people a major issue in the United States. To learn how some others reacted to the issue of women's rights, read the next document on page 111.

Source: Adapted from Elizabeth Cady Stanton, Susan B. Anthony, and Matilda Joslyn Gage, eds., *History of Woman Suffrage*, Volume 1. New York: Fowler & Wells, 1881.

Opposition to Women's Rights

from the *New York Herald*, 1850

After women delegates were not allowed full participation at the World Antislavery Convention in London in 1840, some of them began to meet to discuss the rights of women. After the Seneca Falls Convention in 1848, a number of women's rights conventions were held every year. The press reported on these meetings from a variety of differing viewpoints. What is the viewpoint expressed in the excerpt from the New York Herald, *below, which appeared after the national convention in 1850? In this editorial, the Herald singles out Lucy Stone, Antoinette Brown, and Harriot K. Hunt, who were key women's rights leaders of the time.*

What do the leaders of the women's rights convention want? They want to vote and **hustle** with the rowdies at the polls. They want to be members of Congress, and in the heat of debate **subject** themselves to **coarse jests** and indecent language. They want to fill all other posts which men are ambitious to occupy, to be lawyers, doctors, captains of vessels and generals in the field. How funny it would sound in the newspapers that Lucy Stone, pleading a cause, took suddenly ill in the pains of **parturition** and perhaps gave birth to a fine bouncing boy in court? Or that Rev. Antoinette Brown was arrested in the pulpit in the middle of her sermon from the same causes and presented a **"pledge"** to her husband and the congregation; or that Dr. Harriot K. Hunt while **attending** a gentleman for a fit of **gout** . . . found it necessary to send for a doctor, there and then, and to be delivered of a man or woman child, perhaps twins. A similar event might happen on the floor of Congress, in a storm at sea or in the raging tempest of battle, and then what is to become of the woman legislator?

hustle: mix
subject: expose
coarse jests: rude jokes

parturition: childbirth

"pledge": here used to mean the newborn child
attending: taking care of
gout: disease that causes painful swelling, often in the arms or legs

After 1860 the women's rights movement took a backseat as the country became involved in the Civil War. In the late 1800s women became active once again in fighting for their rights. Opposition to full equality for women continues today.

Source: Eleanor Flexner, *A Century of Struggle.* New York: Atheneum, 1973.

UNCLE TOM'S CABIN

by Harriet Beecher Stowe, 1852

Uncle Tom's Cabin by Harriet Beecher Stowe first appeared in a weekly newspaper in 1851. In 1852 it was published as a book and quickly became a bestseller. Why do you think so many people were anxious to read it? In this excerpt from the novel, a slave named Eliza has just learned that her master has decided to sell her baby to a slave trader named Haley. In response, Eliza escapes with her baby from the plantation in the middle of the night. Mr. Haley has pursued her, along with two slaves named Sam and Andy, who have done their best to mislead him as to where Eliza might have gone.

In consequence of all the various delays, it was about three quarters of an hour after Eliza had laid her child to sleep in the village tavern that the party came riding into the same place. Eliza was standing by the window, looking out in another direction, when Sam's quick eye caught a glimpse of her. Haley and Andy were two yards behind. At this crisis, Sam **contrived** to have his hat blown off, and uttered a loud and characteristic **ejaculation**, which startled her at once; she drew suddenly back; the whole **train** swept by the window, round to the front door.

contrived: managed, usually according to some plan
ejaculation: shout
train: group

A thousand lives seemed to be concentrated in that one moment to Eliza. Her room opened by a side door to the river. She caught her child, and sprang down the steps towards it. The trader caught a full glimpse of her, just as she was disappearing down the bank, and throwing himself from his horse, and calling loudly on Sam and Andy, he was after her like a hound after a deer. In that dizzy moment her feet to her **scarce** seemed to touch the ground, and a moment brought her to the water's edge. Right on behind her they came; and, **nerved** with strength such as God gives only to the desperate, with one wild cry and flying leap, she **vaulted sheer** over the **turbid current** by the shore, on to the raft of ice beyond. It was a desperate leap,—impossible to anything but madness and despair; and Haley, Sam, and Andy instinctively cried out, and lifted up their hands, as she did it.

scarce: hardly

nerved: given courage
vaulted sheer: jumped completely
turbid current: muddy water

The huge green fragment of ice on which she alighted pitched and creaked as her weight came on it, but she stayed there not a moment. With wild cries and desperate energy she leaped to another and still another cake;—stumbling,—leaping,—slipping,—springing upwards again! Her shoes are gone,—her stockings cut from her feet,—while blood marked every step; but she saw nothing, felt nothing, till dimly, as in a dream, she saw **the Ohio side**, and a man helping her up the bank.

the Ohio side: of the Ohio River

When Eliza crossed the Ohio, she reached freedom in the North. The man who helped her up the bank was one of many white people who helped enslaved people escape. Stowe wrote this novel as a protest against the Fugitive Slave Law, which required Northerners to return escaped slaves to their masters.

Source: Harriet Beecher Stowe, *Uncle Tom's Cabin.* New York: New American Library, 1981.

CIVIL WAR PHOTOGRAPHS

by Mathew Brady, 1860–1865

The Civil War was the first war to be documented by photographers. Mathew Brady (1823–1896) was a pioneer of American photography. In 1844 he opened his own studio in New York City. When the Civil War broke out, Brady was on the scene to capture unforgettable images of the politicians and soldiers in the throes of the great conflict. His still photographs of President Lincoln, Jefferson Davis, and Generals Grant, Lee, and McClellan are priceless portraits that show the characters of the men who conducted the Civil War. If this war were being fought today, what kinds of media would be used to document events?

Ulysses S. Grant

Robert E. Lee

Historians and filmmakers continue to use Mathew Brady's photographs from the Civil War era. Brady's original work is housed in the Library of Congress in Washington, D.C.

Source: *Mr. Lincoln's Camera Man, Mathew B. Brady*, Roy Meredith, New York: Dover Publications, 1974.

Battle of Fredericksburg, 1863. First actual photo of the United States Army in combat.

The Emancipation Proclamation

by Abraham Lincoln, 1863

The War Between the States began as a fight to save the Union. Issued by President Lincoln on January 1, 1863, the Emancipation Proclamation refueled the war spirit of both North and South. The year before, Congress had passed a law that freed Confederate slaves who entered Union territory. Now, the Emancipation Proclamation freed those slaves under Confederate rule as well. After the war the 13th Amendment to the Constitution (December 18, 1865) ended slavery throughout the nation. The Proclamation gave strength to the North, which gained over 500,000 former slaves for the war effort and helped secure the support of England and France. What other changes did this decree announce?

Whereas, on the twenty-second day of September, in the year of our Lord one thousand eight hundred and sixty-two, a proclamation was issued by the President of the United States, containing, among other things, the following, **to wit:**

Whereas: since, because

to wit: namely

That on the first day of January, in the year of our Lord one thousand eight hundred and sixty-three, all persons held as slaves within any State, or designated part of a State, **the people whereof** shall then be in rebellion against the United States, shall be **then, thenceforward**, and forever free; and the Executive Government of the United States, including the military and naval authority thereof, will recognize and maintain the freedom of such persons, and will do no act or acts to **repress** such persons, or any of them, in any efforts they may make for their actual freedom.

the people whereof: where the people

then, thenceforward: at that time and in the future

repress: stop

That the **Executive** will, on the first day of January **aforesaid**, by proclamation, **designate** the States and parts of States, if any, in which the people thereof respectively shall then be in rebellion against the United States; and the fact that any State, or the people thereof, shall on that day be in good faith represented in the Congress of the United States by members chosen thereto at elections wherein a majority of the qualified voters of such State shall have participated, shall in the absence of strong **countervailing** testimony be deemed **conclusive** evidence that such State and the people thereof are not then in rebellion against the United States.

Executive: the President

aforesaid: already mentioned; meaning here, the year 1863

designate: name

countervailing: opposing

conclusive: final, not to be disputed

Now, therefore, I, Abraham Lincoln, President of the United States, by virtue of the power in me **vested** as Commander-in-Chief of the Army and Navy of the United States, in time of actual armed rebellion against the authority and government of the United States, and as a fit and necessary war measure for suppressing said rebellion, do on this first day of January, in the year of our Lord one thousand eight hundred and sixty-three, and in accordance with my purpose so to do, publicly proclaimed for the full period of 100 days

vested: placed, given

from the day first above mentioned, order and designate as the States and parts of States wherein the people thereof, respectively, are this day in rebellion against the United States, the following, to wit:

Arkansas, Texas, Louisiana (except the parishes of St. Bernard, Plaquemines, Jefferson, St. John, St. Charles, St. James, Ascension, Assumption, Terre Bonne, Lafourche, St. Mary, St. Martin, and Orleans, including the city of New Orleans), Mississippi, Alabama, Florida, Georgia, South Carolina, North Carolina, and Virginia (except the forty-eight counties designated as West Virginia, and also the counties of Berkeley, Accomac, Northampton, Elizabeth City, York, Princess Anne, and Norfolk, including the cities of Norfolk and Portsmouth), and **which excepted parts** are for the present left precisely as if this proclamation were not issued.

which excepted parts: those areas listed in parentheses

And by virtue of **the power** and for the purpose aforesaid, I do order and declare that all persons held as slaves within said designated States and parts of States are, and henceforward shall be, free; and that the Executive Government of the United States, including the military and naval authorities thereof, shall recognize and maintain the freedom of said persons.

the power: i.e., as President

And I hereby **enjoin** upon the people so declared to be free to **abstain from** all violence, unless in necessary self-defense; and I recommend to them that, in all cases where allowed, they labor faithfully for reasonable wages.

enjoin: order, request
abstain from: not take part in

And I further declare and make known that such persons of suitable condition will be received into the armed service of the United States to **garrison** forts, positions, stations, and other places, and to man vessels of all sorts in said service.

garrison: guard

And upon this act, sincerely believed to be an act of justice, **warranted** by the Constitution upon military necessity, I invoke the considerate judgment of mankind and the gracious favor of Almighty God.

warranted: justified, allowed

In witness whereof, I have hereunto set my hand and caused the seal of the United States to be affixed.

In witness whereof, I have hereunto set my hand: To show what I intend to do, I have written this

Done at the city of Washington, the first day of January, in the year of our Lord one thousand eight hundred and sixty-three, and of the independence of the United States of America the eighty-seventh.

By the President: Abraham Lincoln
    William H. Seward, Secretary of State.

By drawing former slaves North, the Emancipation Proclamation directly bolstered the Union armed forces. Thousands of African Americans joined or worked for the Union army or navy, and helped bring about its victory in 1865.

Source: Abraham Lincoln, *The Emancipation Proclamation.* Reprinted in *The World Book Encyclopedia, Vol. 6.* Chicago: World Book, Inc., 1993.

Destruction of the South

by Eliza Frances Andrews, 1864

Fierce fighting during the Civil War left much of the South in ruins. In November 1864 General William Tecumseh Sherman and 60,000 Union soldiers began a march from Atlanta, Georgia, to Savannah, Georgia, aiming to destroy everything in their path. In the following journal excerpt from December 1864, a Georgia woman named Eliza Frances Andrews (1840-1931) describes some of the destruction they caused. How does Andrews feel about the damage done to the South?

About three miles from **Sparta** we struck the "Burnt Country," . . . and then I could better understand the **wrath** and desperation of these poor people. I almost felt as if I should like to hang a **Yankee** myself. There was hardly a fence left standing all the way from Sparta to **Gordon**. The fields were trampled down and the road was lined with **carcasses** of horses, hogs, and cattle that the invaders, unable either to consume or to carry away with them, had **wantonly** shot down to starve out the people and prevent them from making their crops. The **stench** in some places was unbearable; every few hundreds yards we had to hold our noses or stop them with the cologne Mrs. Elzey had given us, and it proved a great **boon**.

The dwellings that were standing all showed signs of **pillage**, and on every plantation we saw the **charred** remains, . . . while here and there, lone chimney-stacks, "**Sherman's Sentinels**," told of homes laid in ashes. The **infamous** wretches! I couldn't wonder now that these poor people should want to put a rope round the neck of every [one of them that] they could lay their hands on.

Hay ricks and **fodder stacks** were demolished, **corn cribs** were empty, and every bale of cotton that could be found was burnt by the savages. I saw no grain of any sort, except little patches they had spilled when feeding their horses and which there was not even a chicken left in the country to eat. A bag of oats might have lain anywhere along the road without danger from the beasts of the field, though I cannot say it would have been safe from the assaults of hungry man. . . .

I saw [soldiers] seated on the roadside greedily eating raw turnips, meat skins, **parched** corn—anything they could find, even picking up the loose grains that Sherman's horses had left.

Sparta: town in central Georgia

wrath: deep anger

Yankee: Southern term for a Northerner

Gordon: town about 30 miles (48 km) from Sparta

carcasses: dead bodies

wantonly: without caring

stench: bad smell

boon: help

pillage: destruction, robbery

charred: burned

"**Sherman's Sentinels**": name for chimneys left standing after Sherman's troops had destroyed the rest of the house

infamous: wicked

hay ricks: haystacks

fodder stacks: stacks of food for livestock

corn cribs: containers for storing corn

parched: dried

General William Tecumseh Sherman's march through Georgia in 1864 weakened the will of many Southerners to keep fighting. On April 9, 1865, the South surrendered, ending the bloodiest war in the country's history. Southerners spent many years rebuilding their war-torn region.

Source: Eliza Frances Andrews, *The War-Time Journal of a Georgia Girl.* Boston: D. Appleton and Co., 1908.

Teaching Freed People

by Charlotte Forten, 1864

Before the 1860s it was against the law to teach enslaved African Americans how to read and write. Some slaves went to school secretly—and illegally— but most were prevented from getting an education. As the world of slavery crumbled during the Civil War, however, one of the first things African Americans did was set up schools and begin holding classes throughout the South. They hired teachers, both black and white, to teach them. One of the first to head south to educate these newly freed people was a 25-year-old African American abolitionist from Philadelphia named Charlotte Forten (1837-1914). Forten arrived at St. Helena, an island along the coast of the area. Forten began teaching at once—to classes sometimes as large as 140 students! Two years later she wrote two magazine articles about her experiences as a teacher. An excerpt from these articles is printed below. According to Forten, how important was education to the freed people of the South?

The first day at school was rather trying. Most of my children were very small, and **consequently** restless. Some were too young to learn the alphabet. These little ones were brought to school because the older children—in whose care their parents leave them while at work—could not come without them. We were therefore willing to have them come, although they seemed to have discovered the secret of **perpetual** motion, and **tried** one's patience sadly. But after some days of positive, though not **severe** treatment, order was brought out of **chaos**, and I found but little difficulty in managing and quieting the tiniest and most restless spirits. I never before saw children so eager to learn, although I had several years' experience in New-England schools. Coming to school is a constant delight and recreation to them. They come here as other children go to play. The older ones, during the summer, work in the fields from early morning until eleven or twelve o'clock, and then come into school, after their hard toil in the hot sun, as bright and as anxious to learn as ever. . . .

consequently: as a result

perpetual: constant
tried: tested
severe: harsh
chaos: confusion

The majority learn with wonderful **rapidity**. Many of the grown people **are desirous of** learning to read. It is wonderful how a people who have been so long crushed to the earth . . . can have so great a desire for knowledge, and such a **capability** for **attaining** it. . . .

The tiniest children are delighted to get a book in their hands. Many of them already know their letters. The parents are eager to have them learn. . . .

They are willing to **make many sacrifices** [so] that their children may attend school. One old woman, who had a large family of children and grandchildren, came regularly to school in the winter, and took her seat among the little ones. She was at least sixty years old. Another woman—who had one of the best faces I ever saw— came daily, and brought her baby in her arms.

rapidity: speed
are desirous of: want to

capability: ability
attaining: reaching

make many sacrifices: give up many things

Charlotte Forten returned home to Philadelphia in 1864. She later became a writer and translator, and also worked for the United States Treasury Department. With the help of teachers like Charlotte Forten, African Americans built hundreds of schools that were open to both black and white students during the period of Reconstruction that followed the Civil War. African Americans also donated more than $1 million to education in the South. The Freedmen's Bureau, an agency of the federal government, also built schools to teach freed people. This vast system of education became one of the major achievements of Reconstruction.

Source: Charlotte Forten, "Life on the Sea Islands," *Atlantic Monthly*, Volume 13, May and June 1864.

INDEX BY *Category*

INDEX BY *Title*

INDEX BY *Author*

ACKNOWLEDGMENTS

(Continued from copyright page)

"The New Colossus" from THE POETRY OF AMERICAN WOMEN FROM 1632 TO 1945 edited by Emily Stipes Watt. © 1977 University of Texas Press, Austin, TX.

"Aztec Poetry from Nahuatl Texts" from 2-RABBIT, 7- WIND retold by Toni de Gerez, © 1971 Toni de Gerez. Viking Press, NY.

"How Raven Made the Tides' from NATIVE AMERICAN STORIES retold by Joseph Bruchac. © 1991 Fulcrum Publishing, Golden, CO.

"Yeh-hsien" from THE ORYX MULTICULTURAL FOLKTALE SERIES: CINDERELLA by Judy Sierra. © 1992 Oryx Press, Phoenix, AZ.

"Timbuktu" by Leo Africanus as quoted in THE PENETRATION OF AFRICA by Robin Hallett. © 1965 Frederick A. Praeger, Inc. NY.

"Michelangelo Buonarroti" by Giorgio Vasari as quoted in VOICES OF THE PAST: READINGS IN MEDIEVAL AND EARLY MODERN HISTORY edited by Hanscom, Hellerman and Posner. © 1965 Frederick A. Praeger, Inc., © 1967 The Macmillan Company, NY.

"Drawings of Roanoke" from AMERICA THE BEAUTIFUL NORTH CAROLINA by R. Conrad Stein, 1990, Childrens Press, Chicago; from THE NORTH CAROLINA COLONY by William S. Powell, © 1969, Crowell-Collier Press, London; and from NORTH CAROLINA by Eugenia Burney. © 1975 Thomas Nelson Inc., New York.

"A Pilgrim's Journal of Plymouth Plantation" from HOMES IN THE WILDERNESS by William Bradford © 1988 Linnet Books, Hamden, CT.

Excerpt from FATHER JUNÍPERO SERRA by Ivy Bolton © 1952 Julian Messner, Inc., New York.

"Paul Revere's Ride" by Henry Wadsworth Longfellow from ANTHOLOGY OF AMERICAN POETRY edited by George Gesner, © 1983 Crown Publishers, Inc. Avenel Books, New York.

"Concord Hymn" by Ralph Waldo Emerson from THE AMERICAN TRADITION IN LITERATURE, ©1981, Random House, New York.

Excerpt from COMMON SENSE: THE RIGHTS OF MAN AND OTHER ESSENTIAL WRITINGS OF THOMAS PAINE, ©1984 Meridian, New York.

Excerpt from JOHNNY TREMAIN by Esther Forbes. ©1943 Esther Forbes Hoskins, renewed ©1971 by Linwood Erskine, Jr., executor of estate. Cornerstone Books.

"Song of Marion's Men" by William Cullen Bryant from ANTHOLOGY OF AMERICAN POETRY edited by George Gesner. ©1983 Crown Publishers, Inc., Avenel Books, New York.

"Washington's Farewell to His Officers" from MEMOIR OF COLONEL BENJAMIN TALLMADGE. ©1968 Arno Press, Inc. The New York Times & Arno Press, NY.

Excerpt from SHH! WE'RE WRITING THE CONSTITUTION by Jean Fritz. ©1987 G.P. Putnam's Sons, New York.

Excerpt from THE FEDERALIST PAPERS by James Madison, Alexander Hamilton, John Jay. ©1961 NAL Penguin.

Excerpt from JOURNALS OF LEWIS AND CLARK, 1805. ©1964 John Bakeless. New American Library.

"Farewell Address" by Andrew Jackson from THE PRINCIPLES OF AMERICAN STATESMANSHIP edited by Francis Newton

Thorpe. ©1909. The Tandy-Thomas Company, NY.

"Last Appeal for Aid" by William Travis from DOCUMENTS OF TEXAS HISTORY. ©1994 State House Press. Austin, TX.

"Follow the Drinking Gourd" words and music by Paul Campbell TRO-©1951 and renewed ©1979 Folkways Music Publishers, Inc., New York, NY.

Excerpt from "The Declaration of Sentiments and Resolutions" as quoted in THE AMERICAN READER. Diane Ravitch, ed. ©1990 Harper Collins Publishers, New York.

"Opposition to Women's Rights" by the New York Herald, as quoted in A CENTURY OF STRUGGLE by Eleanor Fixler. ©1959, 1968, 1972 Atheneum, New York.

Excerpt from UNCLE TOM'S CABIN by Harriet Beecher Stowe (1852). ©1981 NAL, New York.

From MR. LINCOLN'S CAMERA MAN, MATHEW B. BRADY edited by Roy Meredith. ©1974 Dover Publications, New York.

"The Emancipation Proclamation" by Abraham Lincoln, as quoted in the WORLD BOOK ENCYCLOPEDIA, Vol. 6. ©1993 World Book Inc.

Credits

Photography: 8: The New York Public Library. 13: (c) The Smithsonian Institution. 22: Alinari/Art Resource, NY. 32: American Museum of Natural History. 33: l. The Granger Collection; r. The Granger Collection. 34: t. The Granger Collection; b. The Granger Collection. 44: t.r. The Granger Collection; t.m. from the Amercian Revolution: A Picture Sourcebook, Dover Publications, Inc.; b.l., b.r. from 1800 Woodcuts by Thomas Bewick and his School edited by Blanche Cirker and the Editorial Staff of Dover Publications, Dover Publications, Inc. 45: from 1800 Woodcuts by Thomas Bewick and his School edited by Blanche Cirker and the Editorial Staff of Dover Publications, Dover Publications, Inc. 46–47: Historical Pictures Service. 47: m.r. Schomburg Center for Research in Black Culture, New York Public Library, Astor, Lenox and Tilden Foundations. 49: t.l. The Granger Collection; t.r., b.r. Northwind Picture Archives; b.l. Culver Pictures. 54: Massachusetts Historical Society. 82: The Granger Collection. 83: Massachusetts Historical Society. 93: Museum of American Textile History. 110: t.l. Sophia Smith Collection; m. State Archives of Michigan. 113: t.l. The Granger Collection; t.r. Nawrocki Stock Photo Inc.; b. Bettman Archive. 117: Schomburg Center for Research in Black Culture, New York Public Library, Astor, Lenox and Tilden Foundations.

Cover: McGraw-Hill School Division

Illustration: Anthony Accardo 28–30, 62, 97,98, 100, 118; Elliott Banfield 69; Alex Bloch 81, 87; Michael Bryant 109; Kye Carbone 46, 47; Circa 86, Inc. 71, 72; Jim Cummins 27; Grace Goldberg 11, 95; Richard Golueke 107; James Grashow 71, 72; Carol Greger 6, 7; George Guzzi 55; Stephen Harrington 50, 61, 84, 111, 114, 115; Van Howell 67, 75; Liz Kenyon 106; Dan Krovatin 39, 42; Laurie Marks 25; Marty Norman 77, 79, 80; Vilma Ortiz 12, 31; Taylor Oughton 36, 37; Marcy Ramsey 38, 118; Dorothy Reinhardt 19; Cecil Rice 17, 18; Lauren Rosenblum 89, 90; Joanna Roy 96; Phil Scheuer 44, 45; Dennis Schofield 56, 58, 59; Yuri Sirko 47, 103; Wayne Still 10; M. Kathryn Thompson 2; Cornelius Van Wright 15, 16, 92; Vantage Art 21; S. Michelle Wiggins 3, 4–5.

Text Design: Circa 86, Inc.

TEACHING *Strategies*

Teachers share a common goal—to help their students become successful learners who can understand, remember, and apply important knowledge and skills. This important goal is best supported when students are offered a variety of ways in which to learn.

The Social Studies Anthology offers you the rich and varied tools that you need to help your students learn. It includes such diverse sources as diaries, poems, songs, stories, legends, plays, and posters — all of which draw students into the sights and sounds of the places and times they are studying.

You may invite students to explore the Anthology selections in many unique ways— rewriting documents in another genre, dramatizing the selection, creating posters or collages, or writing original poems, stories, and songs. We have provided a strategy for teaching each selection in the Anthology. But these strategies, of course, are only suggestions. You should feel free to teach the selections in any way that you feel is best suited for your own classroom.

A Cassette accompanies the Social Studies Anthology and provides additional support in teaching the documents. Sometimes the recordings reproduce the voices of the people who wrote the selections. A Cassette logo lets you know which selections have been recorded.

THE NEW COLOSSUS

by Emma Lazarus, 1883

Page 2 🔲

Use with Chapter 1, Lesson 1

Objectives

☐ *Recognize how Lazarus's poem helped make the Statue of Liberty a symbol of the United States' commitment to welcoming immigrants.*

☐ *Create a monument about an ideal that is worth honoring.*

Background Information

The Colossus, a huge statue that stood outside the ancient Greek city of Rhodes, was built to celebrate Rhodes's victory in a war. It was made to look like Helios, the god of the sun.

Creating a Monument

After describing what the Greek Colossus was, play the recording of Lazarus's poem on the cassette and have students read along with it. Then ask the following questions. *How are the Statue of Liberty and the "brazen giant of Greek fame" alike?* (Both were built to commemorate an important concept or event; both are large; both represent mighty powers.) *How are they different?* (The Statue of Liberty is a woman; it was built to serve as a symbol of peace and friendship instead of as a monument to a victory in war.) *According to Lazarus, what important American values does the Statue of Liberty stand for?* (welcoming new immigrants and offering them freedom and opportunity)

After dividing the class into pairs of students, challenge students to design a monument that symbolizes an ideal that is important to them. You might also wish to have them construct models based on their designs. Encourage volunteers to share their designs or models with the class.

SAVE THE EARTH (IT'S NOT TOO LATE)

by Professor Rap, 1991

Pages 3–5 🔲

Use with Chapter 2, Lesson 3

Objectives

☐ *Identify some of the many problems that threaten the environment today.*

☐ *Identify ways in which the rap song encourages people to work together to preserve the environment.*

☐ *Write a song about protecting the environment.*

Writing Your Own Song

After students have read the song, play it for them on the cassette. Tell students that in the recording Professor Rap is performing his own song. Lead them in a discussion about the challenge of preserving the environment. Ask students why it is so important to protect the environment and why we should all pitch in to help in this effort.

Ask students the following questions about the song by Professor Rap: *According to the song, what are some of the problems that are destroying the environment?* (garbage, air pollution, pesticides, acid rain) *What are some ways in which people can work together to preserve the environment?* (stop using aerosol cans, start using biodegradable products, clean up litter, recycle goods)

Divide the class into groups of five students. Challenge each group to compose an original song about why the environment must be preserved and what everyone can do to help. Tell students to write the song in any style they choose. Then have each group perform its song for the rest of the class.

NIGHT JOURNEY

by Theodore Roethke, 1941
Pages 6–7 🖭

Use with Chapter 2, Lesson 1

Objectives

- ☐ *Recognize how the poet uses the image of a moving train to help us to see and feel the diverse geography of the United States.*
- ☐ *Write a poem about local landforms and places of interest.*

Writing Your Own Poem

Ask for volunteers to read the poem aloud. Then play the poem on the cassette. Encourage students to close their eyes as they listen and to picture the scenery and movement being described. Lead students to understand how the narrator seems to become a part of the train on which he is riding.

Ask students whether they have ever taken a trip across parts of the United States. Have volunteers describe memorable geographical features that they saw along the way. Then tell students that they will write their own poems about geographical features or parks located in their community. Before students begin writing, ask them to close their eyes and form a mental picture of the place that they will write about. Tell them to think about all the things they would see, hear, and feel if they were sitting in that place. Challenge students to write as descriptively as possible. Encourage volunteers to read their poems aloud to the rest of the class.

AN AMERICAN HISTORY TEXTBOOK IN THE 1800s

by Emma Willard, 1869
Page 8

Use with Chapter 1, Lesson 3

Objectives

- ☐ *Recognize that textbooks have changed over time.*
- ☐ *Rewrite this lesson from the perspective of a person living in the 2090s.*

Background Information

Remind students that a social studies textbook is an example of a secondary source. Tell them that social studies textbooks, like all other textbooks, change over time. One obvious difference is that Emma Willard's textbook was black and white. Most books today are in color. A more important difference is the inclusion today of women and of Americans from many different backgrounds. In the past, most social studies textbooks focused on the history of European American men. Today social studies textbooks try to tell the stories of all Americans.

Rewriting from Another Perspective

After students have read the selection, ask them in what ways the style is similar to that of textbooks that they have read and also how it differs. Ask students why they think these differences exist. Discuss with students how they think social studies textbooks written 100 years from now will compare and contrast with the textbooks of today.

Divide the class into pairs of students. Challenge members of each pair to work together to rewrite Emma Willard's lesson from the perspective of a person living in the 2090s. Encourage students to consider how new inventions might change textbooks. (Textbooks may be on computers; they may include videotapes, holograms, and so on.) Also ask students to consider how the landscape and climate of the United States may be different 100 years from now. Have volunteers share their version of the textbook with the class.

THE BEAUTIFUL DREAM
Navajo Story Told by Lana Semallie, 1976
Page 10

Use with Chapter 4, Lesson 2

Objectives

☐ *Recognize the importance of oral history and storytelling to the cultures of the Navajo and other Native Americans.*

☐ *Write a story with animals as characters.*

Writing Your Own Story

After students have read the selection, ask students the following questions: *According to the story, what is Coyote's personality like?* (sneaky, greedy, a good talker) *What are Porcupine's personality traits?* (cleverness, intelligence) *Why do you think animals were important characters in Navajo stories?* (because animals were important to the way of life of the Navajo)

Ask students to name tales that they know of that are similar in some way to the Navajo story. (Aesop's fables are a good example, as are African stories about Anansi the spider.) Lead students to understand that stories and legends of many different cultures often feature animals as prominent characters whose actions teach us about such things as the use of cleverness, good versus evil, brains versus brawn, and other lessons.

Then challenge students to write their own story using animals as characters. Encourage them to make sure that their story teaches a lesson, such as how good triumphs over evil. Have volunteers read their stories aloud. Then have the class try to guess the lessons of the stories.

AZTEC POETRY FROM NAHUATL TEXTS
Retold by Toni de Gerez, 1971
Page 11

Use with Chapter 3, Lesson 2

Objectives

☐ *Gain a greater understanding of Aztec history from the words of this poem.*

☐ *Draw comparisons with Americans' perspectives of their own history.*

Background Information

This poem—actually part of a sacred dance ceremony—is filled with references that were important to most Aztec in the 1500s. Just as Plymouth Rock, George Washington, and the bald eagle are powerful symbols for us of our own country, so were Tollan, Tlapallan, and quetzal birds to the Aztec.

Linking to Today

Provide background information to students before having them listen to the poem on the cassette. Then have students read the poem. Afterward, ask students to share what they think the poem's main theme is. (People are wishing for the "good old days" when the land was like a paradise and important rulers like Quetzalcoatl were still present.) *What was the environment said to be like back then?* (hugely productive, filled with beautiful birds) *Do things seem to have stayed the same for the Aztec?* (No, those things are described in the past tense.)

Challenge students to think of conclusions Americans often draw when they look back on their own history and compare life 500 years ago to now. (The environment was in better shape; "law and order" was stronger; life was harder.) Then ask how fifth graders living 500 years from now might describe our country today. As a class, use these statements to compose a short poem about life in the United States today from the point of view of those looking back on the past, using a style similar to the Aztec poem.

A LAKOTA WINTER COUNT
by Lone Dog, 1801-1870
Pages 12–14

Use with Chapter 4, Lesson 3

Objectives

- ☐ *Identify the method used by the Lakota to record their history.*
- ☐ *Recognize that there are many ways to record history and the passage of time.*
- ☐ *Have students create a winter count for their own family, school, neighborhood, or state.*

Creating Your Own Winter Count

After students have studied the selection on their own, lead them in an examination of the pictographs. Ask volunteers to tell the class why each of the pictured events would have been important to the Lakota community.

Ask students how Americans record important events today. Then challenge students to create winter counts that depict important events in their own family, school, neighborhood, or state. If students are making a winter count for their family, they may wish to use one pictograph to record an important event that occurred in each year of their lives. Remind students to write a guide that explains the meaning of each pictograph. Ask volunteers to show their pictographs to the rest of the class, and have the class guess what event is illustrated. Finally, create a bulletin board display showing students' winter counts.

FOUNDING OF THE IROQUOIS LEAGUE
by Hiawatha, about 1570
Pages 15–16 🔲

Use with Chapter 4, Lesson 4

Objectives

- ☐ *Identify the peoples that joined together to form the Iroquois League.*
- ☐ *Recognize the significance of the league's creation.*
- ☐ *Rewrite Hiawatha's speech from the perspective of a President of the United States.*

Rewriting from Another Perspective

Remind students that the Iroquois Confederacy is also known as the Iroquois League. After students have read Hiawatha's speech, play it for them on the cassette. Ask students why they think Hiawatha believed it was important to create the league in the first place. *What did each Iroquois people stand to gain by joining?* Students should understand that the member peoples were much stronger as a united group than they were individually.

Then ask students to rewrite Hiawatha's speech from another perspective. Tell them to suppose that they are the President of the United States. They must write a speech to the people of the United States telling them why it is important for the states to remain united. After students have finished writing, ask volunteers to read their speeches aloud to the rest of the class.

HOW RAVEN MADE THE TIDES
Retold by Joseph Bruchac, 1991
Pages 17–18

Use with Chapter 4, Lesson 1

Objectives

☐ *Recognize the importance of storytelling in the daily lives of Native Americans.*

☐ *Design a newspaper spread that addresses "newsworthy" aspects of this story.*

Designing a Newspaper Spread

After students have read the selection, ask them the following questions: *Why was life hard for people before the creation of tides?* (They were hungry because they couldn't gather seafood.) *Why weren't there any tides then?* (An old woman refused to let out the tide-line that controlled the waters.) *How did Raven trick the old woman into letting go of the tide-line?* (At first he pretended he was eating clams, which attracted the woman's curiosity.)

Divide students into groups of four. Challenge them to suppose that they are newspaper reporters assigned to cover this life-changing story of the making of tides. Because it is a story with so many points of view to it, students are to do several articles and illustrations that fill page one of their newspaper. Have students brainstorm the kinds of "angles" they can cover, for example, how tides will change the lives of people, an eyewitness account of Raven's struggle with the old woman, short profiles of the old woman and Raven, how clams and crabs view this new development. Remind students that effective news reports cover the 5 Ws: Who, What, When, Where, and Why.

YEH-HSIEN
Retold by Judy Sierra, 1992
Pages 19–20

Use with Chapter 5, Lesson 1

Objectives

☐ *Recognize similarities and differences between this Chinese folk tale and the European folk tale known as* Cinderella.

☐ *Write an imaginary interview with Yeh-hsien and Cinderella.*

Writing an Interview

After students have read the selection, challenge them to examine how it is similar to and how it is different from the European version of the story of Cinderella. Ask them how such similar stories might have developed in two separate regions of the world. (Versions of the story might have been shared by travelers, or people might have made up the plot independently based on aspects of life that were common in both regions.)

Challenge students to think about what it would be like if Yeh-hsien and Cinderella discussed their stories on a daytime television talk show. *What kinds of questions would the interviewer ask each woman? How might they respond? How would they describe their shared, and unique, experiences?* Divide the class into groups of three and have them write a script for an interview with Yeh-hsien and Cinderella, including both questions and responses. Encourage a few groups to perform their scenarios.

TIMBUKTU
by Leo Africanus, 1526
Page 21

Use with Chapter 5, Lesson 2

Objectives

- ☐ *Appreciate the cultural and economic achievements of a major West African city during its heyday in the 1500s.*
- ☐ *Create a tourist advertisement for Timbuktu.*

Creating Graphics

Have volunteers read the selection out loud to the class. Then ask students to summarize what it was like to live in Timbuktu during the early 1500s. *What kinds of jobs did people have?* (traders, farmers, doctors, crafts workers, judges, merchants, soldiers, priests, other professionals) *What kinds of food did they eat?* (corn, cattle, dairy products)

Divide students into pairs. Tell them to brainstorm what they would have liked about living in Timbuktu and why people might have come to visit the city. Then challenge them to create tourist advertisements or brochures for the city based on their ideas. Encourage them to include catchy slogans and illustrations. Have groups share their work with the rest of the class.

MICHELANGELO BUONAROTTI
by Giorgio Vasari, 1550
Page 22

Use with Chapter 5, Lesson 3

Objectives

- ☐ *Appreciate the dedication and skill of Michelangelo and the values that prevailed during the Renaissance.*
- ☐ *Do library research on key people of the Renaissance.*

Building Knowledge

After students have read the selection, ask them to help you make a list of words that describe the kind of person Michelangelo seems to have been. (master craftsman, perfectionist, bold, hard on himself and others) Encourage students to explain their choice of terms. Discuss with students how these values in some ways typified the spirit of the Renaissance in Europe.

Invite students to learn more about key people during the Renaissance. Working in small groups, students can choose to learn more about Michelangelo, or they can choose another great artist, a scientist, or a writer who lived and worked during that time. Have them use the library to gather information on their topic. Then have them prepare an oral presentation to the class. Encourage them to use visuals and multimedia resources, if available, in their research or presentation.

AN INDENTURED SERVANT IN VIRGINIA
by Richard Frethorne, 1623
Pages 24–25

Use with Chapter 7, Lesson 3

Objectives

❑ *Identify the way in which many Europeans paid for the voyage to the British colonies in North America during the early 1600s.*

❑ *Identify hardships experienced by indentured servants in North America.*

❑ *Recognize the perspective of an indentured servant concerning his new life in North America.*

❑ *Compare his account with the experience of immigrants coming to the United States today.*

Linking to Today

After students have read the selection, discuss with them the hardships faced by Richard Frethorne in Virginia. Students should understand that food, shelter, clothing, and health were constant concerns for all new colonists. Challenge students to think about how immigrants to the United States today might describe life here in their letters to family members back home. Ask students: *In what ways might their letters be different from Frethorne's? In what ways might they be similar?* (There are fewer deadly diseases in the United States today, and food is more plentiful; life continues to be hard for immigrants today, and many are taken advantage of, as Frethorne was; however, for many immigrants life in the United States is still more secure than life in their home countries; language is also a problem for many immigrants today.)

Have students suppose that they are immigrants writing a letter to a family member back home. Their letters should describe the ease or difficulty of finding a job and a place to live and how they are treated by people already living here. Ask volunteers to read their letters to the class.

THE MAYFLOWER COMPACT
Pilgrim Agreement, 1620
Pages 26–27

Use with Chapter 7, Lesson 4

Objectives

❑ *Recognize the importance of self-government.*

❑ *Understand the reasons that the Mayflower Compact was written.*

❑ *Write an imaginary interview with some of the people who sailed on the Mayflower.*

Writing an Interview

Read the original version of the Mayflower Compact aloud to the class. Then have students read the rewritten version to themselves. When they have finished reading, ask students why the Pilgrims thought it was so important to set up a government in their new home. (to keep order and to improve and help preserve the colony) Ask students to think about what life in their community would be like if there were no laws governing how people should treat each other.

Divide the class into groups and challenge students to write an interview with some of the people who sailed on the *Mayflower*. Tell students to be sure their interviews make clear why the Mayflower Compact was written and why the idea of self-government was important to the Pilgrims. For example, the interviewer might ask Miles Standish why laws are needed in the new colony. (Possible answer: Without laws people do not always consider how their behavior affects others in the community.) Remind students that since only men were allowed to sign the compact, their interviews should also include women and children. Have students volunteer to perform their interviews for the class.

REACHING THE AMERICAS
by Christopher Columbus, 1492
Pages 28–30

Use with Chapter 6, Lesson 1

Objectives

- ❏ *Recognize how the perspective of Columbus differed from that of his crew members as they voyaged westward from Spain.*
- ❏ *Recognize Columbus's perspective on the Taino, the Native Americans of Guanahaní.*
- ❏ *Rewrite the story of Columbus's arrival from the perspective of the Taino people.*

Background Information

Tell students that historians estimate that 250,000 Taino lived in the Caribbean region when Columbus arrived in 1492. This number dwindled to 50,000 in 1515 and 500 in 1550. By 1650 all of the Taino were gone. The major causes of death of the Taino were diseases brought from both Europe and Africa and the harsh conditions, including slavery, imposed by European colonists.

Rewriting from Another Perspective

After students have read the selection, have them discuss the different ways in which Columbus and his crew viewed their voyage westward. Ask students: *Why was the crew unhappy and mistrustful of Columbus? How did he respond?* (The members of the crew were afraid that they would never return to Spain; Columbus scolded them and told them that they had to complete their mission.) Then have students describe Columbus's view of the island of Guanahaní and its people. Ask students if they can think of anything in Columbus's diary that may have foreshadowed the harsh treatment of the Taino.

Challenge students to think about how the Taino may have viewed the arrival of Columbus, his ships, and his crew. Tell them to picture what it might have been like to suddenly meet people who look unlike anyone they had ever seen. Have students rewrite the events described in Columbus's journal from the perspective of a Taino observer. Encourage volunteers to share their versions of the journal with the rest of the class.

THE CONQUISTADORS SEARCH FOR GOLD
by an Aztec Eyewitness, 1550s
Pages 31–32

Use with Chapter 6, Lesson 2

Objectives

- ❏ *Describe the conquistadors' seizure of the royal treasures of the Aztec empire.*
- ❏ *Understand the perspective of the Aztec official who observed the Spaniards' actions.*
- ❏ *Rewrite the account in the form of a news report.*

Rewriting in Another Genre

After students have read the Aztec account, ask them to point out ways in which the author revealed his anger about the behavior of the Spanish conquistadors. Have volunteers pick out specific sentences and read them aloud. (Possible answers include: "Their bodies swelled with greed, and their hunger was ravenous; they hungered like pigs for that gold.")

Divide the class into small groups. Have each group rewrite the account in the form of a news report. Encourage students to "interview" other eyewitnesses, such as Moctezuma, a conquistador, and another Aztec citizen. Remind students that an effective news report includes the 5 Ws: Who, What, When, Where, and Why. Also tell them that a news article should include perspectives or points of view of several different people. Have students volunteer to perform their news reports for the class.

DRAWINGS OF ROANOKE
by John White, 1585
Pages 33–34

Use with Chapter 7, Lesson 1

Objectives

❑ *Recognize the viewpoint of one of the earliest European settlers who came to North America.*

❑ *Write an imaginary journal entry describing Native American village life based on White's drawings.*

Writing a Journal Entry

As students view the illustrations, tell them that John White was one of the earliest Europeans to make detailed drawings of North America. These drawings are as close as we can come to seeing our continent as the English settlers of Roanoke did. Direct students' attention to the map that shows ships off the coast of Roanoke. *Why did White show some ships sinking?* (to warn that sailing off the Outer Banks is dangerous) *What are other ships doing?* (heading inland to explore) *What name does White give to the big chunk of land at the right?* (Weapemeoc) *What does that say about White's view of who controls the land?* (He recognizes that non-English people already live there.)

Now turn students' attention to the pictures of Native American villages. Explain that White tried to include a great deal of information about the daily life of the people living around Roanoke—useful tips for English people preparing to become their new neighbors. Challenge students to suppose that they are viewing such a scene firsthand along with White. Direct them to study all of the drawings on these pages. Then ask them to write a journal entry describing what they are seeing. What do villagers eat, and how do they get their food? What kinds of houses do the people live in? How do they dress? What is one chore that children appear to do? How are animals treated? What is the environment of the area like? Encourage volunteers to read their journal entries to the class.

LIFE ON A NEW ENGLAND FARM
by Ruth Belknap, 1782
Pages 36–37 🔲

Use with Chapter 8, Lesson 1

Objectives

❑ *Identify the many tasks that women colonists had to perform to feed and clothe their families.*

❑ *Recognize the perspective of a woman colonist regarding country and city life.*

❑ *Act out the poem.*

Using Story Theater

After students have read the poem, play it for them on the cassette. Ask students to name the chores that women colonists had to perform in order to feed their families. (milking cows, baking bread, churning butter, feeding hogs, husking corn) Then have them name the chores required to clothe their families. (washing clothes, spinning yarn) Ask students how Ruth Belknap described life in a town. (She thought town life was much easier than living in the country.) Have them discuss whether they think her point of view was accurate.

Then have the class use Story Theater to act out Belknap's poem. Have several students take turns reading aloud parts of the poem while a group of players performs the actions being described. In addition to playing human roles, players should perform as animals and scenery. When the performance is finished, have students discuss whether performing the poem helped them to understand the life that Belknap described. Ask students if they can think of any ways (for example, the addition of dialogue) in which this Story Theater performance could be improved so that it communicates Belknap's ideas more effectively. Have students stage another performance of the poem which includes these improvements.

A PILGRIM'S JOURNAL OF PLYMOUTH PLANTATION
by William Bradford, 1620
Page 38

Use with Chapter 9, Lesson 1

Objectives

☐ *Appreciate the new opportunities, in addition to freedom of religion, that the Pilgrims found upon arrival at Plymouth, such as abundant natural resources.*

☐ *Make an advertisement for Plymouth.*

Background Information

In this journal entry Bradford noted that practically everything the Pilgrims needed to thrive existed in the area. Fresh water, fish, rich soil, fruit trees, herbs, and vegetables addressed the need for food and water. An abundance of trees contained even more riches. Pine trees were valued as firewood, made excellent ship's masts, and supplied pitch and tar for waterproofing. The hardwood from ash and beech trees made strong tool handles and furniture parts, and black walnut was the wood of choice for making charcoal for gunpowder. Last but not least, sassafras was hugely popular among the English as a cure-all drug, and fetched high prices in England.

Creating Graphics

After students have read the selection, ask them why they think Bradford described the area's natural resources so carefully. Remind them to think about what people had to do to meet basic needs and wants before the invention of grocery stores, indoor plumbing, central heating, plastic containers, and so on. As the discussion becomes more detailed, share the background information above. Then divide the class into small groups of "ad agencies." Challenge them to design a poster-sized ad that shows how the area has what it takes to support a fine lifestyle for new colonists. Encourage groups to include as many detailed examples as possible of how the environment will provide for residents' needs and wants. Then have the groups share their work with the class.

PENN'S WOODS
by Navidad O'Neill, 1996
Pages 39–43

Use with Chapter 8, Lesson 2

Objectives

☐ *Recognize how William Penn's Quaker beliefs shaped Pennsylvania's traditions of religious freedom and justice.*

☐ *Perform the play.*

Performing a Play

After students have read the selection, ask them the following questions: *What kind of a leader was William Penn?* (modest, just, fair) *What kinds of laws did he make for Pennsylvania?* (ones protecting religious freedom, trial by jury, free elections) *How did Penn's Quaker beliefs shape those laws?* (Quakers faced persecution in England, so religious freedom was especially important; Quakers believe in "peaceful coexistence with all mankind," which made Penn want to treat Native Americans fairly.) *How did those laws help make Pennsylvania a special place?* (They stressed freedom and fairness for all.)

Choose volunteers to perform the play's speaking roles. Encourage the rest of the class to play nonspeaking parts—for example, other passengers on the ship *Welcome*; the ship's "rails" (to outline the vessel's boundaries), and the local officials who greet the colonists' arrival. If possible, create scenery. Perform the play for a younger class.

POOR RICHARD'S ALMANACK
by Benjamin Franklin, 1732–1757
Pages 44–45

Use with Chapter 9, Lesson 4

Objectives

☐ *Recognize the importance of almanacs in colonial society.*

☐ *Identify values that were important to colonists as reflected in the sayings from Poor Richard's Almanack.*

☐ *Compare and contrast colonial sayings with sayings that are popular today.*

Linking to Today

Ask students if they have ever seen a modern almanac. Have students list ways in which people today learn many of the facts that were once recorded in colonial almanacs. (newspapers, television, radio, and so on). Have each student, in turn, read aloud a saying from *Poor Richard's Almanack*. Have students work together to "decipher" the more difficult sayings so that everyone can understand them. Discuss with students what the sayings reveal about colonial values and the ideas that people thought were important.

Challenge students to think of sayings that are popular today in the United States. (Possible examples are "No pain, no gain"; "Do the right thing"; "Just do it"; "You can lead a horse to water, but you can't make it drink.") Ask students how these modern sayings are similar to sayings from colonial times and how they are different. Point out to students that the saying "No pain, no gain" is popular today but was actually written by Benjamin Franklin. Have students work in small groups to write sayings in the style of *Poor Richard's Almanack*. Then combine these sayings in a class almanac.

SHIP OF HORRORS
by Olaudah Equiano, 1789
Pages 46–48

Use with Chapter 9, Lesson 1

Objectives

☐ *Recognize some of the horrors that enslaved Africans experienced on their forced voyages to the Americas.*

☐ *Understand the perspective of a West African boy who was forced to make that journey.*

☐ *Write a poem based on the narrative.*

Writing a Poem

After students have read the selection, have volunteers discuss what it might have been like to be kidnapped from your homeland and enslaved. Then ask students to write a poem about Olaudah Equiano's horrifying experience. Challenge them to describe the long and terrible voyage. Ask volunteers to read their poems aloud to the class.

SLAVE SALES
Advertisements, 1700s
Page 49

Use with Chapter 9, Lesson 3

Objectives

- ☐ *Recognize that during the time of slavery, human beings were bought and sold as if they were objects.*
- ☐ *Understand that slave sales took place throughout the American colonies in the 1600s and 1700s, and they continued in the South until the 1860s.*
- ☐ *Write a letter opposing slave-sale advertisements.*

Writing a Response

After students have studied the advertisements, have them discuss how they portray the people who are for sale. Ask students in what ways the advertisements depict human beings as property rather than people. Ask students what they think about people being offered for sale. Have students discuss what it might be like to watch a slave sale.

Divide the class into pairs. Have each pair of students work together to write a letter to the editor of a newspaper. Students should suppose that they live in the 13 English colonies in the 1700s and are writing letters in opposition to the advertisements for slave sales. Encourage students to communicate the idea that the enslaved Africans being sold are people, not property. Have volunteers share their letters with the rest of the class.

FATHER JUNÍPERO SERRA
by Ivy Bolton, 1952
Pages 50–52

Use with Chapter 10, Lesson 1

Objectives

- ☐ *Recognize the personal courage of Father Serra and his determination to carry out missionary work in California.*
- ☐ *Write a true story of personal courage.*

Background Information

Father Junípero Serra and Captain Gaspar de Portolá began their northward journey into California in 1769. Along the way Father Serra— a 19-year veteran of missionary work in North America—kept a journal. In it he wrote that he actually experienced temporary relief from his leg wound due to the muleteer's remedy. The wound, however, would never heal. Nevertheless, Father Serra would go on to found the mission of San Diego on his trip with Portolá, and in years to come he would found many more missions, as he walked throughout the region.

Writing Your Own Story

After students have read the selection, have them discuss what Father Serra's goal was for setting out in the first place. (to begin mission work in California) *Why did Father Serra continue his journey despite his serious medical problems?* (He was very committed to his goal.) Encourage students to share examples of other people that they have read about so far in their textbook or anthology who overcame great obstacles to achieve personal goals. (for example, indentured servants and other immigrants, free or enslaved African Americans)

Challenge students to write a story, using real-life or fictional characters, about a person with great courage. Have them include the person's goal, any hardships faced, how those hardships were overcome, and what it was like to achieve the goal. Ask volunteers to read their stories aloud.

THE BOSTON MASSACRE
from the *Boston Gazette and Country Journal*, 1770
Pages 54–55

Use with Chapter 11, Lesson 2

Objectives

❑ *Understand a colonial printer's perspective on the Boston Massacre.*

❑ *Recognize how the writer's point of view can influence the way in which facts are presented in a newspaper article.*

❑ *Rewrite the article from the perspective of a British journalist of the time.*

Background Information

After the event called the Boston Massacre, colonists angrily demanded that the British troops involved be put on trial for murder. The lawyer who defended the British soldiers was John Adams, the famous patriot who later became the second President of the United States. Adams agreed to defend the soldiers because he felt that they had been victimized by an unruly mob of people. The jury found the captain of the British troops innocent, but two of his men were convicted. However, they received only light punishment.

Rewriting from Another Perspective

After students have read the rewritten version of the newspaper article, have them discuss the point of view of its writer. Ask questions such as the following: *What was his opinion about the event that has come to be known as the Boston Massacre?* (that it was an undeserved, terrible tragedy) *How is the writer's opinion expressed in the article?* (through the words he chooses, such as "bloody massacre" and "terrible tragedy"; through the illustration) Ask students why they think that the illustration of four coffins was included.

Challenge students to rewrite the article from the perspective of a British journalist of the time. Ask students to think about how British coverage of the event might have differed from American coverage.

PAUL REVERE'S RIDE
by Henry Wadsworth Longfellow, 1863
Pages 56–60 🔲

Use with Chapter 11, Lesson 3

Objectives

❑ *Recognize Paul Revere's contribution to the fight for American independence from Britain.*

❑ *Appreciate the personal risks Revere undertook for the American cause.*

❑ *Draw a storyboard dramatizing Revere's ride.*

Background Information

Revere set out close to midnight on April 18, 1775, to spread word that British soldiers were marching out of Boston that night. He had to sneak by the British warship *Somerset* at the outset of his journey, and he was stopped by armed British patrols twice that night. However, he escaped each time and even went on to save a trunk full of secret Patriot documents. Longfellow, however, left out the important fact that Revere's ride was just one part of a united effort by American colonists. Others, for example, received the secret church signals. It was one of his colleagues, not Revere, who reached Concord that night. Revere never said, "The British are coming," but rather, "The Regulars [soldiers] are coming," because most colonists at the time still considered *themselves* British.

Drawing Storyboards with Captions

After students have read the poem, play the cassette and have them outline Revere's ride as described by Longfellow. *What kind of man must Revere have been to carry out such a job?* (brave, good horseman, dedicated to the cause) *What challenges might he have faced on that nighttime journey?* (fatigue, cold, darkness, patrols)

Tell students that they are going to make a movie based on the poem. Tell them that their first job is to make a storyboard, which is like a comic strip complete with captions that shows how directors want their movie to look when it is finished. Encourage students to reflect as much of Longfellow's drama as possible in their storyboards. Have students move about the room to view others' renditions, and create a display of the storyboards when completed.

CONCORD HYMN

by Ralph Waldo Emerson, 1837
Page 61

Use with Chapter 11, Lesson 3

Objectives

- ❏ *Recognize that the Battle of Concord was a major turning point in the birth of the United States.*
- ❏ *Appreciate the legacy of freedom Americans share today as a result of ordinary citizens' sacrifices at Concord.*
- ❏ *Honor the sacrifices that others have made on behalf of an important cause.*

Background Information

On April 19, 1775, Concord's militiamen debated how they should respond to the throng of British soldiers heading toward their town. Their minister, William Emerson, thundered, "Let us stand our ground. If we die, let us die here!" Over 50 years later the minister's grandson, Ralph Waldo Emerson, one of our country's greatest poets, wrote this poem in memory of the men who died during the Battle of Concord.

Building Knowledge

Read the poem together after listening to it on the cassette. Then ask why people gathered in Concord in 1837. (to remember the heroes of the Battle of Concord and to honor the legacy of freedom that they left for their children) Have students name some ceremonies held in their communities. (for example: Veterans Day; Independence Day; Presidents' Day; Martin Luther King, Jr. Day; local ceremonies) *What kinds of things do they honor?* (important events in our history, ideals that our country stands for, people who embodied these ideals or who made important contributions to our country)

Challenge students to think of a person or an event that they think has made a positive impact on the world. Then have them create a program for a ceremony that celebrates both the person or the event and their legacies. These programs might include speeches, songs, dramatizations, and other activities. Encourage students to share their program descriptions with the class.

DECLARATION OF INDEPENDENCE

by Thomas Jefferson, 1776
Pages 62–66

Use with Chapter 12, Lesson 1

Objectives

- ❏ *Recognize why the Declaration of Independence was so important to people in the American colonies.*
- ❏ *Understand why this document continues to be important in the modern world.*

Background Information

Despite the fact that Thomas Jefferson owned slaves, his first draft of the Declaration of Independence included an attack on Britain for its involvement in the slave trade. However, this section was later taken out at the insistence of other members of the Continental Congress. Like Jefferson, many members of the Congress were slave owners. They argued that the declaration would not be approved by the Congress if it included the passage denouncing slavery.

Linking to Today

Have students read the rewritten version of the Declaration of Independence. When they have finished reading it, have them discuss the declaration's historical significance. Ask students how the declaration is similar to the Mayflower Compact. (They both express ideas about the reasons why a government is needed.) *How are these documents different?* (The Mayflower Compact set up a government where none existed; the Declaration of Independence cites the reasons why the existing government was unjust.)

Tell students that for over 200 years people seeking independence in different parts of the world have made reference to the Declaration of Independence. Ask students why they think that the ideas expressed in this document, written in 1776, are still relevant in the twentieth century.

COMMON SENSE
by Thomas Paine, 1776
Pages 67–68

Use with Chapter 12, Lesson 1

Objectives

- ☐ *Understand the arguments for independence from Britain that Thomas Paine made in* Common Sense.
- ☐ *Analyze his arguments in a book review.*

Writing a Book Review

Before reading the selection, tell students to be on the lookout for two major arguments Paine made in favor of independence. One involves a comparison to a child growing up, while the other describes how geography supports the idea of American independence. As volunteers read the selection to the class, clarify any of its more complex words and phrasings. Then ask students: *How does Paine use the example of a child growing up to explain how and why the colonies can thrive apart from Britain?* (Just as a child's diet changes as he or she grows up, so must America's relationship with Britain and the rest of the world.) *How, according to him, does geography work in favor of American independence?* (The colonies' distance and size in relation to Britain confirm that they should be independent.)

Remind students that *Common Sense* became a huge bestseller as soon as it was published in 1776. Challenge them to review the book and its point of view for a colonial newspaper. Recall that, like all good book reviews, their work should provide a short summary of the book's "plot" or point of view as well as their opinion regarding whether that point of view is well expressed and worth reading.

JOHNNY TREMAIN
by Esther Forbes, 1943
Pages 69–70

Use with Chapter 12, Lesson 2

Objectives

- ☐ *Understand the conflicting emotions colonists felt toward Britain on the eve of the Revolutionary War.*
- ☐ *Compare and contrast the status of the Continental and British armies at the beginning of the Revolutionary War.*
- ☐ *Rewrite the scene as a newspaper article.*

Rewriting in Another Genre

After students have read the selection, ask them to describe the overall scene taking place in the excerpt. (British troops are moving out toward Lexington, where the Revolutionary War will begin.) *Why is Johnny divided in his feelings about Britain?* (Its heritage of liberty gave birth to the colonists' own struggle; Johnny, like others, still feels British in heritage but feels even more an American.) *Why does "Yankee Doodle" seem to have almost no hope of succeeding against the "great scarlet dragon"?* (The British are much better armed and trained.)

Tell students to suppose that they are colonial news reporters and have just interviewed Johnny Tremain for an article on the dispatch of British soldiers to Lexington. Remind them to address the 5 Ws of journalism: *Who, What, Where, When,* and *Why.* Encourage students to include a comparison of the British and American armies. Have volunteers read their articles to the class.

A PETITION FOR FREEDOM
by African Americans of Massachusetts, 1777
Pages 71–72

Use with Chapter 12, Lesson 2

Objectives

- ☐ *Recognize the perspective of African Americans on the Declaration of Independence.*
- ☐ *Compare and contrast the petition with the Declaration of Independence.*
- ☐ *Write a letter to the editor of a newspaper explaining why the practice of slavery is in conflict with the ideas expressed in the Declaration of Independence.*

Writing a Letter

Have students read through the petition on their own. Afterward, lead them in a line-by-line reading, stopping to define difficult words along the way. Then have students compare the petition with the Declaration of Independence. Ask a volunteer to read aloud the rewritten version of the second paragraph of the Declaration of Independence. Ask students how the ideas expressed in this paragraph conflict with the existence of slavery. (The declaration states that all men are created equal, that liberty and the pursuit of happiness are unalienable rights, and that governments are designed to protect these rights.) Students should understand that the African American writers of the petition agreed with the ideas expressed in the Declaration of Independence but believed that the declaration should apply to all people.

Challenge students to suppose that they are living in 1776. Have each student write a letter to the editor of a newspaper explaining why slavery is wrong, according to the ideas expressed in the Declaration of Independence. Have volunteers read their letters aloud to the class.

SONG OF MARION'S MEN
by William Cullen Bryant, 1831
Pages 73–74 🔲

Use with Chapter 12, Lesson 3

Objectives

- ☐ *Appreciate the battle tactics and bravery of Francis Marion and other Southern patriots.*
- ☐ *Produce an imaginary television news report on Marion and his soldiers.*

Background Information

In the final years of the Revolutionary War, Francis Marion and his soldiers led devastating attacks against British forces along South Carolina's Santee River. His bold acts made him a hero whose fame was almost as great as George Washington's. Villages named themselves Marion in his honor, and today there are 17 counties throughout the country that still bear his name.

Rewriting in Another Genre

Lead students in reading the poem, asking volunteers to help you explain difficult phrases or words. After listening to it on the cassette, have students discuss why Marion's nickname, "the Swamp Fox," was well chosen, according to Bryant. Encourage them to use lines from the poem to bolster their opinions.

Divide the class into groups, then challenge them to suppose that they are television reporters sent back in time to make "Marion's Men" the "People of the Year" on their news broadcast. Tell them that, as topnotch journalists, their reports should cover the 5 Ws: *Who, What, When, Where,* and *Why.* Also encourage them to include brief visuals ("footage") of the men "in action" and interviews, if possible—all within about three minutes. Have each group deliver their report to the class.

WASHINGTON'S FAREWELL TO HIS OFFICERS

by Benjamin Tallmadge, 1783
Pages 75–76

Use with Chapter 12, Lesson 3

Objectives

☐ *Appreciate the great devotion Americans felt toward George Washington because of his leadership during the Revolutionary War.*

☐ *Create a farewell card for Washington.*

Creating Graphics

Before students read the selection, ask them to describe someone in their lives that they greatly admire. *What makes that person great?* Ask them how they would react if they were told that they would no longer have any contact with their hero or heroine. Now tell them to read the selection.

After students have finished reading, encourage them to share their impressions of what kind of man and leader George Washington was, based on what happened in the selection. Challenge them to suppose that they are to be one of the well-wishers present at Washington's farewell. Ask them to create a good-bye card to him. Have volunteers share their work with the class or use it in a class display.

SHH! WE'RE WRITING THE CONSTITUTION

by Jean Fritz, 1987
Pages 77–81

Use with Chapter 13, Lesson 2

Objectives

☐ *Recognize the serious issues the Constitutional Convention debated, such as how much power should be given to the federal government and how much should be given to the state governments.*

☐ *Conduct a debate on the issues discussed in the selection.*

Background Information

To get a sense of how powerful state rather than national identity was at the time, it is interesting to note that throughout the 1700s and early 1800s Americans often said, "The United States *are…*" rather than "The United States *is…*" It wasn't until after the Civil War that people commonly referred to the country as a single unit, rather than as a union of individual states.

Conducting a Debate

After students have read the selection, ask them to explain why the term "national government" created such a huge debate at the Constitutional Convention. (It implied that the new government would be supreme over the states.) *Why do you think this issue was so important?* (They had fought a war to win the right to rule themselves, and they didn't want to be controlled again by a large, powerful government.) *Why did some representatives dislike the idea of having one person be head of the government?* (It was too much like monarchy.)

Divide the class into an even number of small groups. Have pairs of groups debate each other on one or more of the issues discussed in the selection. Allow the groups time to plan the arguments they will make before holding the debate. Encourage them to anticipate what arguments the other side will make so they can be prepared to counter them. Then allow each side five minutes to make their case and five minutes to refute the opposing side. You might also wish to have the class read and discuss the excerpt from *The Federalist* on page 84 before holding the debate.

TWO VIEWS ON WOMEN'S RIGHTS
by Abigail Adams and John Adams, 1776
Pages 82–83

Use with Chapter 13, Lesson 1

Objectives

- [ ] *Understand Abigail Adams's perspective on women's rights.*
- [ ] *Understand John Adams's perspective on women's rights.*
- [ ] *Compare and contrast these perspectives.*

Background Information

Early American women had very few legal rights. They could not vote, and their educational opportunities were limited. When they got married, women lost the right to own property; anything owned at the time of their marriage became the legal property of their husbands. At the time of the American Revolution, the only people permitted to vote were white men who owned land. Most women, African American and Native American men, and white men who did not own land were barred from voting.

Conducting a Point/Counterpoint

Lead students in a reading of all three letters. Ask volunteers to explain particularly difficult passages. Then have students discuss how the opinions of Abigail Adams and John Adams differed. (Abigail Adams felt that if men truly believed in independence, they would extend equal rights to women; John Adams suggested that if men gave up any control, they would be subject to the rule of women.) Ask students: *Why did these differences exist?* (Abigail Adams knew from experience what it was like to be treated as a second-class citizen.) *Do you think that John Adams was entirely serious in his reply? Why or why not?*

Tell students that all Americans have equal rights under the law today, but that women did not receive the right to vote nationally until 1920. Ask students to suppose that they are living in the late 1700s. Have them suggest reasons that all Americans should be able to vote.

THE FEDERALIST, NUMBER 10
by James Madison, 1787
Page 84

Use with Chapter 13, Lesson 4

Objectives

- [ ] *Recognize fears people had about what the Constitution might do to the idea of representative government.*
- [ ] *Determine that James Madison's point of view was that our government would be fairer with a larger number of representatives.*
- [ ] *Rephrase his argument in modern-day terms.*

Background Information

Once the Constitutional Convention ended, Americans began to fiercely debate the proposed plan of government. New York's Governor George Clinton summed up many people's fears when he charged that the Constitution was "a license for the rich to plunder the poor." Since the Constitution called for just a few people to represent the interests of the entire country, what would stop rich and powerful people from buying the votes of representatives and effectively taking over? Federalists, or supporters of the Constitution, responded to Anti-Federalists' fears in a flurry of newspaper articles. In this excerpt from one article, James Madison argued that republican government works most fairly on a big rather than a small scale, because special-interest groups have a harder time gaining majority control.

Linking to Today

Share background information with the class before helping them read through the document. *In this excerpt what main argument does Madison make against small republics?* (A large number of representatives would help prevent "cabals," or elite or special-interest groups, from taking over.) Challenge students to sum up Madison's point of view in their own words. Tell them that this debate is still going on today, as some politicians push for smaller government or less government control, and greater control by the states. How might this issue apply to a debate over whether classroom-sized or school-sized representation would be fairer to students' interests?

ESCAPE FROM WASHINGTON
by Dolley Madison, 1814
Pages 86–87

Use with Chapter 14, Lesson 3

Objectives

❑ *Recognize Dolley Madison's courage during the War of 1812.*

❑ *Understand why it is useful to read firsthand accounts of historical events.*

❑ *Draw a storyboard dramatizing Dolley Madison's experience.*

Drawing Storyboards with Captions

After students have read Dolley Madison's letter, have them discuss how she reacted to her situation. Lead students to understand that remaining in the President's House for so long required great courage. Have students discuss how reading a firsthand account is different from reading about historical events in a textbook. Ask students: *Why is it useful to read a firsthand account?* (Firsthand accounts present a vivid and memorable portrait of the events being described; they tell us how people felt at the time.) *Why is it important to read explanations of events written after they occurred?* (Accounts of events that are written later are in some ways a more accurate summary of what occurred as they are less influenced by the writer's own point of view.)

Then have students suppose that they are going to make a movie of Dolley Madison's experience. Tell them that the first thing they need to do as filmmakers is to create a storyboard of the action, complete with dialogue. A storyboard is a type of comic strip that shows how film directors want their movie to look before it is shot. Encourage students to make their storyboards as detailed, dramatic, and realistic as possible and to create a working title for their film. Each storyboard should have several different panels showing different events in the order in which they occurred. Have volunteers share their storyboards with the rest of the class.

THE JOURNALS OF LEWIS AND CLARK
by Meriwether Lewis, 1805
Page 88

Use with Chapter 14, Lesson 2

Objectives

❑ *Appreciate the rigors involved in Lewis and Clark's exploration of western North America.*

❑ *Trace their route to the headwaters of the Missouri River.*

Background Information

Meriwether Lewis began his epic journey in July 1803 by traveling overland from Washington, D.C., to Pittsburgh. From there he boarded a boat headed down the Ohio River and picked up William Clark and others at Louisville, Kentucky. The little group continued on to the point where the Mississippi and Ohio rivers converge; from there they headed up the Mississippi to St. Louis, a trading post founded by the French near the place where the Missouri flows into the Mississippi. There they stayed for five months in order to prepare for the hardest part of their journey. In May 1804 the Lewis and Clark expedition to the Pacific Northwest began in earnest.

Tracing a Route

After students have read the selection, ask them why they think Lewis was so careful to note so many directions and mile markings in his journal. (so others might follow in the future) *Why were expedition members so happy to reach the start of the Missouri River?* (One of the expedition's goals was to explore the Missouri, and it had taken them over a year to reach its source.) *What did Lewis and his group do after leaving the Missouri?* (headed further west, connected with another river, which he called the Columbia)

Divide the class into groups of two. Challenge them to trace as much of Lewis's journey as possible from an atlas map. (Note: the group didn't immediately hook up with the present-day Columbia River; they followed the present-day Lemhi, Salmon, and Snake rivers to the Columbia.) Have them note which present-day states the expedition traveled through as well as what the terrain was like along the way.

THE REMOVAL OF THE CHEROKEE

by John G. Burnett, 1890
Pages 89–90

Use with Chapter 14, Lesson 4

Objectives

- [ ] *Recognize the tragedy of the Trail of Tears, the forced relocation of the Cherokee from the Southeastern United States to Oklahoma.*
- [ ] *Understand Burnett's feelings about the injustice of the Trail of Tears.*
- [ ] *Dramatize Burnett's account through Story Theater.*

Using Story Theater

After students have read Burnett's account, have them discuss why they think that Burnett called this "the blackest chapter on the pages of American History." Ask students: *How would you have reacted if you had been a Cherokee? How would you have reacted if you had been a soldier ordered to participate in the removal of the Cherokee?*

Then have the class act out Burnett's account through Story Theater. Have several students take turns reading aloud parts of the account while a group of players performs the actions being described. "Lead roles" include the parts of Chief John Ross, Ross's wife, President Andrew Jackson, and Burnett himself. When the performance is finished, have students discuss how performing the story helped them to understand the tragedy of the Trail of Tears.

FAREWELL ADDRESS

by Andrew Jackson, 1837
Page 91 ▣

Use with Chapter 14, Lesson 4

Objectives

- [ ] *Identify Andrew Jackson's point of view regarding why he was about to force Native Americans from their lands in the Southeast.*
- [ ] *Write a response to Jackson's point of view.*

Writing a Response

After reading the selection to the class, have students listen to the speech on the cassette. Then ask them: *What is President Jackson's view of how life in the United States had fared under the Constitution?* (The country had gone through hard times, but it had "preserved unimpaired the liberties of the people.") *Who are some people who hadn't done as well as they could, in his view?* (people in states with Native Americans and Native Americans themselves) *According to Jackson, how would forced removal benefit both groups?* (White settlers would finally be able to prosper; Native Americans would be moved to a safe spot, would be placed under "the paternal care" of the government, and would be "civilized.") *In this view are all Americans equal and equally entitled to life, liberty, and the pursuit of happiness?* (No, Native Americans are considered to have fewer rights and lesser abilities.)

Challenge students to write a letter to President Jackson responding to his point of view regarding Native Americans and their land. Encourage them to use facts from their textbook and anthology to disprove his views that Native Americans are "uncivilized" and would be better off giving their land up to more "deserving" Americans.

THE FACTORY BELL
by an Unknown Factory Girl, 1844
Pages 92–93 🔊

Use with Chapter 15, Lesson 1

Objectives

- ❑ *Recognize how the poem helps us to understand the life of a worker in an early American factory.*
- ❑ *Recognize how the poet uses bells to illustrate the hard life of a factory worker.*
- ❑ *Compare the work of a young woman in an early American factory to the work of young people today.*

Background Information

From the 1820s until the late 1840s, women from New England made up a large portion of the industrial work force in the United States. During the 1840s, however, factory owners began to hire thousands of men and boys from Irish immigrant families who had come to the United States to escape a terrible famine. These men and boys began to do much of the factory work that previously had been done by women. To factory owners, time was money, and workers were forced to work long hours for very little pay.

Linking to Today

After students have read the poem, play it for them on the cassette. Have them discuss why the author may have chosen a bell to symbolize the new industrial way of life. (Life was no longer regulated by the cycles of nature but by clocks and bells.)

Have students discuss how their own lives are shaped by clocks and bells. Then challenge them to write a schedule of a typical day, including the times that they wake up, go to school, have classes, eat meals, do homework, play, and go to bed. Ask volunteers to share their schedules with the rest of the class. Finally, ask students to compare the hours they spend in school and doing homework to the work hours of a worker in an early American factory.

LAST APPEAL FOR AID
by William Travis, 1836
Page 94

Use with Chapter 15, Lesson 3

Objectives

- ❑ *Understand the unequal battle lines that were drawn when Texans sought to defend the Alamo during their war for independence from Mexico.*
- ❑ *Create an imaginary television news report on the Battle of the Alamo.*

Background Information

In February 1836 a force of around 200 Texans led by William Travis barricaded themselves in the Alamo, despite Texas General Sam Houston's order to abandon San Antonio. When Mexico's General Antonio López de Santa Anna surrounded the old fort with about 5,000 men and demanded that the Texans surrender, Travis answered with cannon fire. He also dispatched a secret messenger to the Texas government with this last appeal for aid. No aid ever came. On March 6 Santa Anna's forces stormed the Alamo and, despite huge losses, retook the fort. No Texas soldier survived the fight.

Rewriting in Another Genre

After students have read the selection, ask them to describe in their own words what was happening around the Alamo as Travis wrote this document. *Why was it clear that the Texans were in serious trouble?* (The Mexicans had more firepower and soldiers.) *Why do you think the Texans fought so fiercely despite overwhelming odds against them?* (They felt strongly about their bid for independence.)

Divide the class into small groups. Tell them to suppose that they are television news crews assigned to produce a three-minute report on the showdown brewing at the Alamo. Challenge them to include short "interviews" with soldiers from opposing sides, "live footage" of the two sides facing off, and commentary on what the battle is all about and why it is important. Have each "news crew" perform its report for the class.

ERIE CANAL
Traditional Song, 1800s
Page 95 📼

Use with Chapter 15, Lesson 2

Objectives

☐ *Identify how the song conveys what it was like to work on the Erie Canal.*

☐ *Compare and contrast transportation via the Erie Canal with transportation today.*

☐ *Trace the route of the Erie Canal.*

Background Information

Although the Erie Canal was a tremendously important trade route in the 1800s, its design was surprisingly simple. The canal was only 4 feet (1m) deep and about 30 feet (9m) wide. Canal boats were towed by mules that were guided along a path running alongside the canal. At best, the boats could travel 4 miles (6 km) per hour. Towns often built bridges across the canal. These bridges were sometimes so low that the people riding on boats were forced to lie flat as they passed underneath.

Tracing a Route

After students have read the lyrics of the song, play it on the cassette. The version on the cassette includes a second verse. Ask students: *How is the transportation of goods today different from the way goods were transported in the past?* (Today goods are transported much more quickly, mostly by trucks, ships, and planes.) Lead students to understand that the transportation of goods continues to be essential to the economic health of the United States.

Divide the class into pairs of students. Have each pair work together to locate the route of the Erie Canal using the maps on pages 413 and R12–R13 of their textbook. Have students write the answers to the following questions: *Where are Albany and Buffalo, and on which two bodies of water are they located?* (Albany is on the Hudson River in eastern New York; Buffalo is on Lake Erie in western New York.) *How did the canal make it possible for goods from Ohio and Michigan to be shipped to New York City?* (Goods were carried east by boat across Lake Erie, through the Erie Canal, and south on the Hudson River.)

SWEET BETSY FROM PIKE
Traditional Song, 1800s
Page 96 📼

Use with Chapter 15, Lesson 5

Objectives

☐ *Appreciate a popular song sung by "Forty-Niners" and other cross-country travelers.*

☐ *Rewrite the song as a news article that highlights the struggles and dreams of overland travelers.*

Rewriting in Another Genre

Use this activity after students have read the next selection, *Diary of an Overland Journey to California.* After students have read the song, play it for them on the cassette. Afterward, have them compare Ike and Betsy's fictional experience with Sallie Hester's real-life experience on the overland trail. Ask students: *How were these experiences similar?* (traveling along the Platte River; crossing prairies, wide rivers, and tall peaks; physical hardship and setbacks along the way) *Why do you think that "Sweet Betsy from Pike" was so popular among travelers?* (Lead students to understand that adding humor to a story can make difficult real-life experiences easier to bear.)

Have students suppose that they are news reporters assigned to write an article on the struggles and dreams of travelers heading west. Challenge them to rewrite "Sweet Betsy from Pike" as a news article. Remind students that unlike a song, news articles should stick to the facts. Have volunteers share their articles with the class.

DIARY OF AN OVERLAND JOURNEY TO CALIFORNIA
by Sallie Hester, 1849
Pages 97–100

Use with Chapter 15, Lesson 5

Objectives

- ☐ *Recognize how Sallie Hester's diary describes the difficulty of crossing the United States in 1849.*
- ☐ *Identify challenges faced by Sallie Hester and her family during their journey.*
- ☐ *Draw a storyboard of Sallie Hester's trip.*

Drawing Storyboards with Captions

Have students take turns reading parts of the diary aloud. Then have students use the map on page 99 to trace Sallie Hester's journey. Have students discuss what they think would have been the most difficult, most fun, most exciting, and most boring parts of the journey westward. Ask students: *What skills and personal qualities did travelers need in order to survive?* (courage, perseverance, strength, patience) *What forces beyond their control contributed to their success or failure?* (diseases, accidents, lack of water)

Tell students that they will make a video of Sallie Hester's journey. Divide the class into groups of five students. Have each group create a storyboard with captions showing scenes from their video. All of Sallie Hester's diary entries should be illustrated on the storyboards of each group. Encourage students to show how the landscape changed as Sallie Hester traveled west across the United States. Have a spokesperson from each group present its storyboards to the rest of the class.

SLAVERY DEFENDED
by George Fitzhugh, 1857
Page 102

SLAVERY DENOUNCED
by Frederick Douglass, 1852
Pages 103–104 🔲

Use with Chapter 16, Lesson 1

Objectives

- ☐ *Understand why a former slave and a slave owner had different perspectives on slavery.*
- ☐ *Compare and contrast these perspectives.*

Conducting a Point/Counterpoint

After students have read the two selections, play Douglass's speech on the cassette. The version on the cassette, read by the renowned actor Ossie Davis, varies slightly from the version in the text. Then have students discuss the views of each writer. Ask students: *What accounts for the writers' differences in perspectives on slavery?* (Fitzhugh used captive African Americans to work his plantation; his livelihood depended on slavery and the misconception that blacks were inferior to whites; Douglass had lived through the cruelty of slavery and had firsthand knowledge of its horrors.) *Which of the selections presents an accurate view of slavery?* (Douglass's) *Which of these two men had the best understanding of how it felt to be enslaved?* (Douglass, because he had spent 21 years of his life in slavery)

Ask students how Frederick Douglass might have reacted to George Fitzhugh's defense of slavery. Then have them write a letter responding to Fitzhugh. Tell students to refer to Douglass's own experiences in slavery. Ask volunteers to read their letters aloud to the class.

FOLLOW THE DRINKING GOURD

Spiritual, 1800s
Pages 105–106 [cassette icon]

Use with Chapter 16, Lesson 2

Objectives

❑ *Appreciate the role of "code songs" such as "Follow the Drinking Gourd" in the lives of enslaved African Americans.*

❑ *Trace a route enslaved people could follow to freedom along the Ohio River.*

Tracing a Route

Play the song for students on the cassette once through. Then play it again and have students follow the lyrics carefully. Ask students: *How do you think the fact that the secret directions were hidden in a song helped more people to learn those directions?* (The words to songs are often easier to remember than straight text; moreover, singing can be a faster way to spread information than whispering from one person to the next.)

Remind students that the "old man" described three rivers as leading toward freedom in the North: the Tombigbee, Tennessee, and Ohio rivers. Divide the class into pairs of students and challenge them to locate these three rivers on an atlas map. Then have them list all the slave and free states that these rivers passed through. Have students analyze how these geographic facts might have affected the flow of human traffic on the Underground Railroad.

DECLARATION OF SENTIMENTS AND RESOLUTIONS

Declaration of the Seneca Falls Convention, 1848
Pages 107–108

Use with Chapter 16, Lesson 2

Objectives

❑ *Understand that American women were denied basic human rights in the 1800s.*

❑ *Appreciate the efforts of women such as Lucretia Mott and Elizabeth Cady Stanton to improve the status of American women.*

❑ *Outline and interpret the main ideas of the declaration.*

Building Knowledge

Divide students into pairs. Have one turn to the Declaration of Independence, on page 62, and the other to the Declaration of Sentiments and Resolutions. Ask students the following questions: *How does the Declaration of Sentiments and Resolutions compare to the Declaration of Independence?* (The Declaration of Sentiments and Resolutions mirrors much of the format and wording of the Declaration of Independence.) *Why do you suppose that the two documents are so similiar?* (The authors of the Declaration of Sentiments and Resolutions felt that, because they were women, they were being denied basic rights, like the colonists were.) *How are the two documents different?* (The Declaration of Independence deals with the subject of independence from Britain and leaves out any reference to women.) Remind students that like the Declaration of Independence, the Declaration of Sentiments and Resolutions contains a list of grievances.

Ask students to read the Declaration of Sentiments and Resolutions silently. Then have each pair create a summary of its points on poster paper. When the groups have finished their work, have them present their findings to the class.

"AIN'T I A WOMAN?"
by Sojourner Truth, 1851
Pages 109–110 🔲

Use with Chapter 16, Lesson 2

Objectives

☐ *Understand Sojourner Truth's perspective on women's rights as a woman who was once enslaved.*

☐ *Compare Sojourner Truth's speech to the letters of Abigail Adams.*

Background Information

When Sojourner Truth was born in New York in 1795, she was named Isabella van Hardenbergh. After the end of slavery in New York State in 1827, she changed her name. "My name was Isabell," she said, "but when I left the house of bondage, I left everything behind." She chose the name Sojourner Truth because she felt that God was calling her to sojourn, or "travel up and down the land," to spread the word of truth. She spent the rest of her life traveling around the Northern states giving speeches against slavery and in support of women's rights.

Building Knowledge

After students have read the speech, play it for them on the cassette. Ask them to describe Truth's message in their own words. (Truth was making the point that women had proven that they were equal to men; she asserted that women would take the rights that they deserved.) Ask students why a woman who had once been enslaved might have a different perspective on women's rights than men and women who had always been free. (Enslaved women were forced to engage in physical labor that was harsher than the work of even very poor free men and women. While enslaved, Sojourner Truth had endured hardships that would have been difficult for any person, man or woman.)

Have students reread the letters of Abigail Adams on pages 82–83. Have students write a paragraph comparing and contrasting these letters to the speech by Sojourner Truth. Ask volunteers to read their paragraphs aloud to the rest of the class.

OPPOSITION TO WOMEN'S RIGHTS
from the *New York Herald*, 1850
Page 111

Use with Chapter 16, Lesson 2

Objectives

☐ *Acknowledge the arguments some Americans used in the 1800s to oppose equal rights for women.*

☐ *Write a response to the arguments.*

Writing a Response

Have volunteers read the selection to the class. Then ask students: *According to the writer, what did leaders of the women's movement want?* (to vote, run for office, become doctors or lawyers) *Why, according to the writer, were women unsuited for these things?* (They were too busy having and caring for babies and would be subject to language inappropriate for women.)

Now lead students in a comparison of this source's point of view with the points of view of the two previous anthology selections. *What do they share in common?* (the subject of women's demands for the vote and for equality in other ways as well) *What point of view do the two previous anthology selections share?* (They both support women's rights, including full equality and the right to vote.) Ask students to write a letter to the editor of the *New York Herald* in which they respond to the arguments set forth in this selection. Remind them to refer to points made in the previous two selections. Have volunteers read their letters to the class.

UNCLE TOM'S CABIN
by Harriet Beecher Stowe, 1852
Page 112

Use with Chapter 16, Lesson 3

Objectives

- ☐ *Appreciate the tragedy of slavery as portrayed in one of the most influential abolitionist writings of the time.*
- ☐ *Create a book cover for the novel.*

Creating Graphics

After students have read the selection, ask them to sum up what happens in this excerpt from the book. *What role does Sam play in the attempt to recapture Eliza?* (He makes a loud noise to warn Eliza that Haley is coming after her and, by creating a distraction, gives her time to run away.) *Why does Sam side with Eliza even though he's working for the slave trader Haley?* (As an enslaved person himself, he empathizes with her plight.) *How does the author make you feel about Eliza?* (You're on her side and want her escape to freedom to succeed.) *Why do you suppose this book was such a powerful document for the abolitionist movement?* (It gave slavery a human face and showed how unjust the institution was to enslaved people.)

Divide students into pairs. Challenge them to create a book cover for *Uncle Tom's Cabin* that will revive interest in the book among people today. Remind students that book covers have eye-catching graphics as well as descriptions of the book's plot and explanations of why it is an important publication. Quotes by famous people about the work are also common. Have teams inspect each other's work.

CIVIL WAR PHOTOGRAPHS
by Mathew Brady, 1860–1865
Page 113

Use with Chapter 17, Lesson 1

Objectives

- ☐ *Appreciate the real-life nature of the Civil War that Mathew Brady caught on film.*
- ☐ *Plan an historical photoessay.*

Background Information

Photography had only been in existence for 21 years when the Civil War broke out. In those early years film consisted of large plates of glass that had to be dipped in chemicals and slowly exposed while the liquid was still wet. Although plagued by very poor vision, Mathew Brady became one of the United States' earliest and most successful photographers. When the Civil War broke out, he devoted his wealth and expertise to capturing the war on film. He hired about 20 other photographers to help in this effort—but the country's gain was Brady's loss. Brady was nearly bankrupted by his Civil War project, and he died a poor man in 1896.

Planning a Photoessay

After students have examined the photographs, ask them how the pictures help them get a better feel for what it was like to live and fight during the Civil War. *What kinds of details from the pictures make the war or the time especially real?* (the kind of clothes worn, the kinds of equipment used, the emotions and activities depicted) Encourage students to suppose that they are responsible for photographing an important historical event. Working in small groups, have them choose an event or time period and make a list of the people, places, and events they would need to photograph in order to provide a comprehensive picture of what things were like. Have each group share their lists with the class and obtain feedback on what else they might include or what they might delete.

THE EMANCIPATION PROCLAMATION
by Abraham Lincoln, 1863
Pages 114–115

Use with Chapter 17, Lesson 2

Objectives

- [ ] *Understand that the Emancipation Proclamation led to the end of slavery in the Southern states.*
- [ ] *Summarize the document's main points in the form of a newspaper report.*

Rewriting in Another Genre

After students have read the document, have them discuss why it sparked such a major turning point in American history. (It called for the end of slavery.) Ask them: *Did the proclamation immediately free all slaves?* (No, technically it freed just those in states still in rebellion against the United States; an amendment to the Constitution in 1865 would outlaw slavery for good.) *What else did the proclamation do?* (It called for the recruitment of African Americans as Union soldiers.)

Encourage students to suppose that they are newspaper reporters who have just covered Lincoln's delivery of the proclamation. Challenge them to write a short news report about the new document. Remind students that an effective news report includes as many of the 5 Ws as possible—*Who, What, When, Where,* and *Why.* Finally, tell students to add a suitable headline to their story.

DESTRUCTION OF THE SOUTH
by Eliza Frances Andrews, 1864
Page 116

Use with Chapter 17, Lesson 3

Objectives

- [ ] *Recognize a Southern woman's perspective on the destruction caused by General Sherman's army.*
- [ ] *Write an essay on Sherman's march and its place in American history.*

Background Information

Eliza Frances Andrews, born in Washington, Georgia, was the daughter of a highly respected judge. In the stormy years before the Civil War, Judge Andrews and his wife supported those who wanted the Southern states to remain with the Union, while Eliza and her brothers sided with the secessionists. Eliza secretly sewed a Confederate flag that was raised when Georgia seceded from the Union. As he watched this celebration, Eliza's father commented, "Poor fools! They may ring their bells now, but they will wring their hands— yes, and their hearts, too—before they are done with it."

Building Knowledge

After students have read the selection, have them share their reactions to the destruction caused by Sherman's march. Ask students how they would react if an enemy army did the same thing to their homes and community. Tell students that some people think that the devastation caused by Sherman's army was necessary in order to end the war and abolish slavery. To this day some people consider Sherman a hero, while others view him as a barbarian.

Have students write an essay, based on the information contained in this selection and in the textbook, about the place of Sherman's march in American history. Help students to recognize how different perspectives on the war can affect people's views of General Sherman. Have volunteers read their essays aloud to the class.

TEACHING FREED PEOPLE
by Charlotte Forten, 1864
Pages 117–118

Use with Chapter 17, Lesson 4

Objectives

☐ *Understand how Charlotte Forten's magazine article makes clear the desire for education among former slaves.*

☐ *Recognize the sacrifices that these people were willing to make for education.*

☐ *Rewrite Forten's article from the perspective of a student in her classroom.*

Rewriting from Another Perspective

After students have read the selection, have them point out examples in the article that indicate how important education was to former slaves. (Children came to school after a hard day's work in the fields and were eager to learn; many adults came to school and made sacrifices so that their children could attend.) Ask students: *How was Forten's class different from classes today?* (Her classes were much bigger; students ranged from little children to grandparents; people made sacrifices to come to school, which was not mandatory as it is today.)

Challenge students to rewrite Forten's magazine article from the perspective of a student in her class. Remind students that until slavery was abolished, African Americans in the South were forbidden to learn how to read and write. Tell students to explain in their article why education is so important and what it means to be able to learn to read and write at last. Have volunteers share their articles with the rest of the class.